FROM THE MULL TO THE CAPE
A GENTLE BIKE RIDE ON THE EDGE OF WILDERNESS

RICHARD GUISE

summersdale

FROM THE MULL TO THE CAPE
Copyright © Richard Guise, 2008

Faulkner, James Donal, 'Ullapool: Nach Bog An Latha?' (unpublished). © James Donal Faulkner 1996. With permission.

Groome, Francis Hindes (editor), *Ordnance Gazetteer of Scotland* (originally 1882, Thomas C. Jack). Included in www.geo.ed.ac.uk/scotgaz/gaztitle.html (Gazetteer for Scotland, a gazetteer of Scottish towns and villages), which is © The Editors of the Gazetteer for Scotland 2002–2006. With permission.

Various, The Statistical Accounts of Scotland (1791–9 and 1834–45). www.edina. ac.uk/stat-acc-scot. © the University of Glasgow (www.glasgow.ac.uk) and the University of Edinburgh (www.ed.ac.uk). With permission.

Summersdale Publishers Ltd
46 West Street
Chichester
West Sussex
PO19 1RP
UK

www.summersdale.com

Printed and bound in Great Britain

ISBN 13: 978-1-84024-674-2

To my father, Ron Guise (1910–2007), also a cyclist

Acknowledgements

Thanks to Maxim Alexander, Julie Challans, Jim Faulkner, Ronald Guise, Niall MacKinnon, Tim McEwan, the Meteorological Office, David O'Donoghue, Ian Slingsby, Jennifer Teague and Kevin Ward. Thanks also to all at Summersdale who have helped convert my raw material into a readable book, especially Lucy York and Carol Baker.

Contents

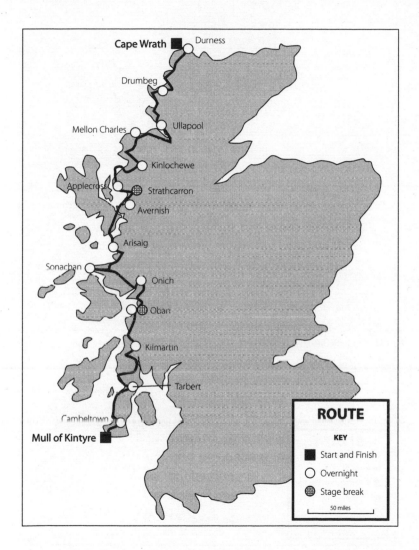

Cape Wrath ■ Durness

Drumbeg

Mellon Charles ● Ullapool

Kinlochewe

Applecross ⊕ Strathcarron

Avernish

Arisaig

Sonachan

Onich

⊕ Oban

Kilmartin

Tarbert

Campbeltown

Mull of Kintyre ■

ROUTE

KEY

■ Start and Finish

○ Overnight

⊕ Stage break

50 miles

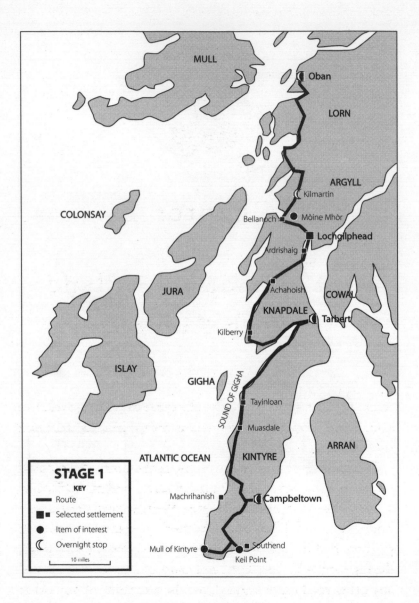

MULL

COLONSAY

JURA

ISLAY

GIGHA

ATLANTIC OCEAN

LORN

Oban

ARGYLL

Kilmartin

Bellanoch ■ ● Mòine Mhòr

Lochgilphead

Ardrishaig

Achahoish

KNAPDALE

COWAL

Tarbert

Kilberry

SOUND OF GIGHA

Tayinloan

Muasdale

KINTYRE

ARRAN

Machrihanish

Campbeltown

Mull of Kintyre ● ■ Southend

Keil Point

STAGE 1

KEY
━━ Route
■■ Selected settlement
● Item of interest
☾ Overnight stop

10 miles

Chapter 1

That Dreaded Headland: South Kintyre

'Och, yer show-off!' the lady selling me the sausage roll had said. 'I can show it you on a wee postcard here an' save you the bother.'

This had seemed an odd response at the time. What could be less bothersome for a Saturday afternoon in April than a little bike ride beside the sea? Well, it was now a few hours later and I'd had 'the bother'. The last six miles to get here had turned out to be less bike ride than bike push, during which I'd lost sight not only of the sea but also of any other road users. Indeed, for the last hour, of any other human. The heavy hills, darkened by the remains of last year's heather, had been closing in on all sides around the single-track road as I pushed my bike to a weary halt where progress was blocked by a locked gate with a faded yellow sign announcing in barely legible letters: 'WARNING: THIS HILL IS DANGEROUS'. As if the previous six miles hadn't been.

I left the bike on the safe side, jiggled on foot through the narrow gap and stepped onto a grassy knoll to the right of the tarmac. And there it was. While, at the same time, there it wasn't.

There was the lighthouse: a distant, white, stumpy building at the end of a ragged line of old-fashioned telegraph poles. There, a fair distance below the light, was the choppy grey of the North Atlantic, stretching to a hazy horizon, where lurked two shapes. The darker one lay on the sea like a brooding alligator: Rathlin Island. To its left a distant, hazier shape rose steeper and wider, hinting at a larger island beyond: Ireland.

What did not seem to be there was what I'd set out to reach today, what the sausage-roll lady had wanted to show me on a postcard instead: the Mull of Kintyre.

★

Sitting cross-legged on the knoll, I pulled her squishy snack out of my bag and, munching eagerly, examined the map in the plastic pocket on the bag's top. If you can force the strains of 1970s bagpipes to the back of your mind for a moment, let me put the Mull of Kintyre into context. On a map of Scotland's west coast, Kintyre is the long, thin peninsula dangling over Northern Ireland like the ugly, misshapen nose of an old cartoon witch. The tip of her nose is the Mull, barely twelve miles from Ireland. The one sizeable drip from the nose is Sanda Island to the east... and I think perhaps we'd better leave the nasalogy there. To get here I'd taken two ferries, with Arran as a giant stepping stone in between, from Ardrossan in Ayrshire to Claonaig on Kintyre, cycling down the quiet but beautiful east coast and staying overnight in Campbeltown. That morning's ride had taken in the village of Southend, home of the sausage-roll lady, and the push up to the Mull.

And what is a mull? Er, um, now let me think... and apart from that it's a promontory, of course. Now that I looked at the map again, I had to admit that a tough route might have been expected: the six-mile track to the Mull did cross from white area to brown area quite quickly and did end up near an impressive spot height of 428 metres at Ben na Lice, impressive since zero metres was only about a mile away. This rose on my right as a high, impenetrable wall of dark moss and heather. But where was the Mull? I'd expected a windy, Flamborough-type headland with grand, 360-degree views over the North Channel and Kintyre. Well, on my left lay an even more massive lump of the same glowering undergrowth, sturdy and solid, blocking the view and saying, I now realised, 'Hey, dunderhead, it's me – I'm the Mull.'

Ah, yes. Now looking at the map for the umpteenth time, I recognised that the track signposted to the Mull didn't actually mount the thing, but sneaked alongside it for a mile or two before veering off towards the lighthouse. I was sitting as near as you could get to the Mull of Kintyre without actually diving into the Atlantic and crashing against its cliffs. This would do for my purpose, which was to travel the length of the Highlands from their south-west corner, here at the Mull of Kintyre, to their north-west corner at Cape Wrath in Sutherland, 264 miles away as the crow flies – or as a crow mad enough to make such a journey would fly. As an extra challenge, wherever it was viable I intended always to take the route closest to the coast, thus making my route considerably longer than the mad crow's: probably around 600 miles. ('Viable' to be defined en route.) I reckoned I'd be able to do it in three stages.

And why was I doing this? Well, firstly I just needed a project. Since retiring from proper work a few years before, I'd dipped my toes into those activities you always promise you'll indulge in when you finally step off the nine-to-five treadmill – trace family tree, learn guitar, tidy attic, save world – but somehow none held my attention for long. None was exactly a physical challenge. When a friend only slightly younger than me had launched himself into the London Marathon, I decided I'd better do something marathonian myself before it was too late. A few years before, I'd done one of those subtropical charity bike rides without too much bodily torment and so a bike ride it would be.

Secondly, it was simply the standard daydream of a suburban Sassenach. Being regularly engulfed by road traffic or jostled by market-day shoppers naturally plants in us a desire to be elsewhere, with grass and rock underfoot, a big sky above and nothing much else around.

Thirdly, it was because of a recent fascination with the Scottish Highlands. Four or five brief visits over as many years – for a wedding, an eclipse and visiting friends – had revealed that this part of Britain felt quite different from the rest, a land apart that I'd like to understand a bit better.

Oh, and the west coast of Scotland just happens to be the most spectacularly beautiful place in the world. On a good day.

*

I creaked to my feet and wandered around the little hillocks sipping my still vaguely warm coffee and searching in vain for a view of anything but the lighthouse.

The 1882 *Ordnance Gazetteer of Scotland*, edited by F. H. Groome, described the Mull of Kintyre as 'that dreaded headland… whose precipices breast the full swing of the Atlantic'. Spot on.

In his 1959 book *The World's Lighthouses Before 1820*, David Alan Stevenson noted in reference to the Mull of Kintyre lighthouse that it was built high above the sea, inaccessible from it and barely more accessible by land. Even spotter on.

The Northern Lighthouse Commissioners, established in 1786, identified the Mull of Kintyre as one of the earliest sites to warrant a lighthouse, no doubt with a mind to the loss of so many lives in recent shipwrecks during the violent storms of 1782. The light first operated in 1788. It was rebuilt in a more permanent form as early as 1830, began using electricity in 1976 (Highlanders being somewhat conservative in adopting new fads) and was automated only in 1996. From this I infer that until only ten years before my visit, someone actually lived and worked out here. I hope the duty roster was tolerable.

Jiggling back through the gap, I walked over to an information board standing next to the empty parking spaces. It reminded me of the many aircraft that have also failed to make it past this dangerous headland, including a Chinook helicopter in 1993 in which several senior British Intelligence officers died. Nearby, it said, is a memorial to this recent tragedy, but with no clues as to whereabouts this 'nearby' was. I really should have scouted around to pay my respects, but this lonely spot was already giving me the creeps and, keen to get the trip under way, I packed away my bits and pieces, swung a leg over the bike and, with my mind set on another lighthouse at Cape Wrath in faraway Sutherland, pushed off.

It didn't take long to get into the rhythm again. *Da-di-da-daa, oh mist rolling in from the da-di-da-daa…* Actually, Paul McCartney's former Highland hideaway isn't on the Mull at all, but in the hills to the north of Campbeltown – more of him and it tomorrow. Right now, my next port of call was to be Keil Point, where a popular idol from another time reputedly first set foot in Scotland.

The First Law of Cycle Touring is:

1: What goes up must come down.

I'd struggled up and so I was looking forward to freewheeling back down to the real world. The sheep had other ideas. Time after time I'd get up speed only to squeeze on the brakes ten centimetres from the behind of a retreating sheep. I know it's not their fault they have small brains, but the lesson that would help their roadside survival is surely a simple one: off tarmac = good, on tarmac = bad; or, if they don't know what tarmac is: green underfoot = safety, black underfoot = danger. And yet what do they do when a vehicle joins them on the road? Run further along the black stuff. It was April and plenty of lambs were also trotting along, failing to learn the same lesson. On one painfully slow sheep-sheep-bike parade down a long incline, two little lambs broke away from their mother and ran in the opposite direction towards me, forcing a complete stop. As my foot went from pedal to road, the two disobedient little rascals nuzzled each side of the front wheel, until Mum baaed them both into the ditch and let me pass. Now, if they couldn't even distinguish their mother (white, woolly, four legs) from a man on a bike (yellow and black, two wheels) then I didn't much rate their chances of surviving even long enough to provide a decent Sunday lunch.

Eventually, I was able to freewheel happily, reeling in the isolated features I'd passed two hours before – the last/first farmhouse, the last/first human still chainsawing some logs, the last/first red Fiesta parked in a yard and covered in mud – until, at a farm called Druma Voulin, I emerged on a road that actually carried other traffic. My route beckoned left, but I turned right to Keil Point.

When I say someone 'set foot' in Scotland I mean it literally, for the guidebooks say his footprint, reputedly made some 1,400 years ago, is visible right there in the rock at Keil Point. Intrigued as to why anyone should step onto molten rock at any time, let alone seconds after surviving a hazardous sea journey, I was keen to take a look.

A sign announcing the footprint pointed at a gate. I locked my bike and continued on foot through a small field of inquisitive sheep and past a wishing well. The path ran parallel to a cemetery and then petered out on a hillside. Must have missed it. Retracing my steps but finding no more clues, I leaned over the wall of the cemetery, but there was no way in except from the road. I even peered into the wishing well in case the print were among the handful of ten-pence pieces that lay on the bottom: nothing foot-shaped. Standing hands on hips, I outstared the sheep. Well. Dark clouds were beginning to gather over the sea, the sheep were no help at all and I was no fan of Colum Cille's, whose foot it allegedly was.

So I unlocked, remounted and set off again, defeated. As I was pedalling back onto the coast road, a party of six religious-looking types (three neat beards, three sensible skirts, six white smiles and twelve bright eyes) emerged from nowhere and passed through the gate into the sheep field, feeding the beasts with handily prepared snacks. I bet they found the footprint.

Cille by name...

Colum Cille was born in AD 521, a grandson of King Niall of Ireland. He was a Christian and held a treasured copy of the Gospels, while the king was not and endeavoured to relieve his grandson of the tome. Colum resisted, the king insisted and, well, this being Ireland and the subject being religion, things went from family quarrel to bloody battle before you could say 'Father Ted'; the upshot being that, as a self-imposed penance for having been the cause of such bloodshed, Colum departed for Scotland in 563. Nobody seems sure why he felt Scotland would be such a punishment – the pipes maybe?

So, apparently, Colum Cille and his maritime entourage landed at Keil Point, where (apparently) the distraught chap turned around to note that he could still see his wretched Ireland and thus (apparently) cast off again, sailing round the Mull and eventually up to Iona, an island far enough north for the irksome Emerald Isle not to be visible. All these 'apparently's seem appropriate for such vague history from so long ago – after all, since you could see Kintyre from Ireland, even a sixth-century geographical dunce might have figured out that you could also see Ireland from Kintyre.

Not satisfied with the trouble he'd already caused, Colum didn't simply settle quietly on Iona amid the cows, frogs and snakes, but rather banished these beasts from the island. Along with all the women. He then decided to use this beautiful but frog-free island as a base from which to shoot about Scotland converting everything that moved to Christianity, for which effort his friends dubbed him Saint Columba.

Back at Druma Voulin, where farmer and tractor were being pursued across a field by a hundred noisy seagulls, I faced my first choice. The road to Campbeltown and Mrs Mac's B&B was straight on, but The Rule – that I should always take the road nearest the west coast – would take me on a diversion up Glen Breackerie to the left. The weather was now closing in. I was a bit saddle-sore. With two failures already behind me (the memorial and the footprint), I didn't feel much like breaking The Rule so early on, and so I pulled out my little radio, plugged in the earphones and set off up the glen.

To begin with it was pleasant cycling territory indeed: lazy green meadows, safely distant sheep, busy farmyards, flat road and Radio Five Live – for the football updates. Apart from me, nothing much moved along the narrow lane, until my team scored and a small flock of bright yellow siskins burst out of the ditch to join my sudden celebration.

As the ground began to rise, I pedalled on along the strangely smooth surface that eventually entered a forest of evergreens and turned north-east, bringing a stiff breeze into my face and interrupting my radio reception. A drop of rain fell through a slit in the helmet. Then another. And another. Hat. I didn't bring a hat! Why I'd thought a cycle helmet with slits would keep out the rain I don't know. It was raining quite hard now. Shelter. I can sit it out. But the road was bordered by newly dug ditches with nowhere to cross them. I realised now it was a logging road: great for trucks but no nooks and crannies for cyclists. Waterproof trousers. I'd better get them out of my bag. Dismounting in the middle of the deserted road, I tried to open my bag while propping up the bike. In vain. All I was doing was getting myself and the contents of my bag wetter.

I mounted up again and skidded round another bend that put the wind behind me, flapping something against my neck. What's that? Ah, all cagoules have hoods! Idiot. Stop again, pull hood over helmet, set off again. A big drip dangled from the helmet's peak, while a bigger drip pedalled away beneath.

Over a small rise Radio Five came back, this time bringing bad news to match the worsening weather. Stopping yet again under a small branch that reduced the rainfall by about one per cent, I unplugged the radio and disconsolately shoved it into a dripping pocket. Surveying the scene of ragged grey clouds scraping soggy green fields, I decided it was time for a little mental adjustment. This was just rain, just water. It's what you get in Scotland. I was out in the fresh air – OK, perhaps a little over-fresh – scooting about in new territory, getting some great exercise and, most of all, at the start of an adventure! Would the Famous Five be downhearted just because the weather was a bit iffy and their team losing? They would not. They'd be looking ahead to a scrumptious tea after they'd dried themselves off on warm, fluffy towels. So, shaking off the latest collection of puddles from my cagoule's crinkly corners, I squished off again whistling a merry tune. Ha, I whistle in the face of your Scottish rain! Even as it seeps into my weak English brain.

The route I was taking – north from the coast where Ireland and Great Britain are closest – was also a route taken about 1,800 years before by the Gaels.

Gaels blowing in from the south-west

I like a good bit of irony. The territory I was traversing would nowadays be regarded as on the economic and political fringes of Scotland, whose power base is firmly entrenched in the Central Lowlands. In a sense, however, this is the original Scotland.

Back in the early centuries AD, after the Romans had given up and gone home, the land that is now Scotland comprised four kingdoms. Edinburgh would have fallen in Bernicia, an Anglish kingdom, i.e. occupied by Angles. Glasgow would have been part of Strathclyde, the Celtic Britons' territory that stretched south from the Clyde. The largest kingdom, covering much of the north and all the north-east, was occupied by Celtic Picts and is usually referred to as Pictland.

That left the south-western Highlands and Islands. From about the third century AD, invaders from Ireland had at first raided and then settled this rugged coast. Like the Britons, they were also Celtic and spoke a Celtic tongue. The Irish that came here spoke Gaelic; hence 'Argyll': coastland of the Gaels.

These particular Gaels came mostly from nearby Antrim, where they were known as the Dál Riata and their kingdom as Dalriada. The name transferred with them and so this coastal kingdom was also known as Dalriada. To confuse matters still further – and to bring us back to the point – the departing Romans had referred to the Irish by a word which is thought to have meant 'pirates': they called them the 'Scoti' and their island 'Scotia'. The people of Dalriada were therefore also called Scoti, or Scots.

So when, in 1034, all four kingdoms were finally united under Duncan, the first king of 'all the Scots', it was from the people of Argyll, this area, that the new kingdom took its name: Scotland.

To summarise: the Scots were originally Irish, but not all of Scotland's people were Scots, although almost all were Celts – but not the same type of Celts as the Irish, or Scots. Some of Scotland was Anglish, or English, and some was British – that is, Celtic – until eventually, when British was mostly non-Celtic, it was all British. The Scots, whose name comes

> from Latin, spoke Gaelic, a Celtic language, while most of
> Scotland spoke a different Celtic language or Anglish or
> English, but not Latin.
>   Clear as mud?

Mud was one item I wasn't short of when, an hour and a half
after the rain had started, I squelched into Campbeltown,
splashed through Mrs Mac's car park and lugged the bike
into the ground-floor room I'd left that morning, parking
it on the bath towel. BBC Scotland's *Final Score* teased me
with the exploits of Hearts and Callies before admitting
that my boys had lost at Hartlepool and dropped out of the
top six.

Never mind. At least I'd learned the Second and Third
Laws of Cycle Touring:

2: If it might rain, it will.
3: Know your kit.

*

After a nap, a shower and a dash of Deep Heat, I was
revitalised and ready to hit the town – or the Wee Toon, as
the locals call it. Many guidebooks dismiss Campbeltown
as an ugly, characterless place and I hoped they were
wrong. I really wanted Kintyre's metropolis (population
6,000) to have something about it. Well, it did: it had a
seafront featuring the world's ugliest Woolworths and the
aluminium shelter that Milton Keynes rejected; it had a
very big and very empty harbour; and it had a two-bed flat
in town for only £38,000. It also had a clearing sky and so
I sat in the reject shelter and stared out on a calm sea. The

1882 *Gazetteer* was quite taken by Campbeltown's setting at the head of its 'picturesque and lively bay'. Well, at least it was still picturesque that April evening – as long as you kept looking out to sea.

As I'm sure you'll have noticed while doing the washing-up, the standard tea-towel map of the Highland clans shows the whole of Kintyre to be MacDonald territory; so why is its main town named after their arch-enemies, the Campbells? Well, up to the seventeenth century, the settlement Kinlochkilkerran – 'Ciaran's church by the head of the loch' – was indeed a Campbell stronghold. However, the MacDonalds were not too popular with King James V, who promptly handed the area to the Campbells in the form of the Earl of Argyll. 'Kinlochkilkerran' was far too Gaelic for the earl, who renamed it with all modesty after himself and his clan. Quite when and why Campbeltown lost its second L is a mystery I've been unable to solve.

The Wee Toon's heyday was the nineteenth century with coal, fishing, shipbuilding and whisky all being local boom trades. Alas, it was a dodgy foursome for the twentieth century and even today the town is still recovering from their parallel declines. The town's biggest single employer is now a Danish wind turbine company but, as with other towns in the Highlands, most of its income nowadays comes from tourism... and so a handsome young Englishman, recently arrived on a posh bike, should be a welcome sight. I stood up, turned round and cast myself loose into the Kintyrenean night with a tenner in my pocket. Who would relieve me of it?

The obvious, indeed only, pub on the front was The Royal Hotel. The Scots may be good at lighthouses, bridges and golf, but are notoriously bad at pubs: there's just something odd about almost all of them. The Royal's problem was that you couldn't see inside from out, and so I didn't know whether I'd be the only customer. No go. I'd noticed a row of pubs on a back street that looked like they might have some decent beer among them and sought them out again. With the Scottish ban on smoking in pubs now in its fourth month, busy pubs had knots of smokers shivering around the door in their shirtsleeves. This revealed The Commercial Inn as a popular venue, despite its curtained windows, and so I trolled in.

The names on the pumps meant little to me, and evidently I meant little to the barmaid, but I'd had a fair can of Tennant's at the B&B and so plumped for that. Sitting quietly in the corner with my maps and my pint, I took a sip. Uurgh! Lager. My fault. I did struggle through half, but left the other half on the table as I tried next door: The Wee Toon. Squeezing past the solitary puffer in the doorway, I marched in. Deserted. Not a soul save the bloated and baleful barman watching Liverpool play Chelsea and looking like he supported neither.

'Ah, er, just a half please – whichever's the bitter.'

It was the 70 Shilling. I turned to watch the footie. Uurgh! Bitter it may have been, but also cold and fizzy. Making a mental note to do some research into real ales in Scotland, I rapidly downed the pop and sneaked out when Mr Cheery wasn't looking.

Next along was The Argyll Arms Hotel. Now this certainly had customers, but they all seemed to be fourteen years old, topped with ginger pudding basins and silently staring as though auditioning for *The Village of the Damned*. A banner across the door declared: 'Tonight: Kintyre Piping Society'.

Now hungry as well as thirsty, I trudged over to The White Hart Hotel. Mmm, the food smelled good. Customers were actually cheering at the football, a Chelsea defeat being cause for celebration everywhere. Responding eagerly to my enquiry, the bonhomous barman suggested a pint of Velvet, a lasagne and the table over there with a good view of the match. So I supped the fizzless flagon, which slid nicely down like, well, like velvet. I may have failed with the footprint, but had survived the weather and had now succeeded in tracking down a decent pint in Kintyre – not a bad Day One, all in all.

Chapter 2

Happy Isthmus: West Kintyre

Both Sunday and I dawned bright and breezy and so before breakfast I nipped down to the newsagent's to get a quick dose of the beautiful local accent.

'Good morning! The local newspaper please.'

'G'day. Yeah, thit'll be the *Kimbletown Kyurier*.'

Wondering what might have attracted an Aussie to this grey old town, I strolled back to the digs and, over my flakes, set about the *Campbeltown Courier*. Both a leading story and a letter to the editor concerned the proposal to site another huge wind farm up in the hills of Kintyre. According to the letter, the developers admitted they'll kill over 400 birds (a year?) with their turbines, while, according to the news article, the developers' spokesman stated that there was no threat to the birds at all. Someone must have been wrong here. Another story brought the badly timed news that in eight days a new pedestrian ferry service would start up between Troon and Campbeltown – badly timed for me anyway, as it would have saved me and my bike about a day. Mind you, the jaunt across Arran and down eastern Kintyre two days before (to get me to the Mull) had been the sort of spectacular, sunny Scottish cycling I was rather hoping for again today; certainly the weather was promisingly similar.

Drifting in from the kitchen came the BBC news that on her eightieth birthday the Queen had received over 20,000 cards. Drifting in shortly after was Mrs Mac, the landlady: 'Och, she'll nivver read 'em – wha' a waste o' money!' Long live the Scots. (I have rechristened all the landladies I met en route as the ubiquitous Mrs Mac – to save their embarrassment and my head.)

Beflaked, bebaconed and betoasted, I was soon in the saddle again and searching the landscape for signs of something rare in these parts.

The Campbeltown and Machrihanish Railway followed pretty close to the line of my route out of the Wee Toon towards Machrihanish, and I peered over field and hedgerow for a telltale straight line at odds with the natural contours. Nothing obvious as far as Stewarton, where I turned right along a minor road that I was fairly sure crossed the old rail route. An embankment a hundred metres ahead looked promising, but turned out to be a dyke; a mysteriously straight hedge just petered out. No, nothing. Not a sausage. Oh well, at least today's failure had come early in the day.

A unique railway?

The Campbeltown and Machrihanish Light Railway opened in 1887 to carry coal from collieries near Machrihanish on the west coast to a coal depot and pier at Campbeltown on the east. In 1906 the upgraded and no longer 'light' railway began passenger services. Steamers would bring visitors from Glasgow to Campbeltown, there to catch a train to the west coast – perhaps for a quick round of golf at the Machrihanish links – and back again, sometimes completing a return journey the same day. The closure of the collieries in 1929 signalled the demise of the C&M, which finally ceased all operations in 1932.

The most remarkable aspect of what must have been a splendid railway is its location, being, by my reckoning, not only the most remote from any other railway on mainland Britain, but also the only mainland passenger service not actually connected to the rest of the network. The nearest other line, by land, was the Oban terminus of the Caledonian Railway – three days' cycling away.

The next sight on my schedule was surely too big to miss, even for me. Just beyond the missing railway, there emerged from the gorse bushes on my left a long and very well-maintained stretch of barbed wire fencing. Pulling up and standing on tiptoe, I tried to see over the gorse and through the wire to a place where the rolling landscape of Kintyre had been flattened into the unrolling airscape of Machrihanish Airport's runway.

This was a very small airfield with a very long runway. Why? Officially, because until 1997 it was a NATO airbase and part of a vital network of airfields capable of taking even the largest aircraft in an emergency. But unofficially? Well, according to a whole couchload of conspiracy theorists, Machrihanish was – or even still is – a test site for a super-supersonic, and of course super-supersecret, American stealth bomber code-named *'Aurora'*. The evidence offered by the theorists includes:

- the supposed fact that the entire runway was – or is? – painted four times a year 'to match the surrounding undergrowth' so as to be invisible from space (but it's on the OS maps, chaps);
- that a local oil engineer once saw a 'dart-shaped' aircraft that he didn't recognise;
- that the chairman of Scottish Earth Mysteries Research once breathlessly revealed that southern Kintyre would be an ideal spot for secret research as it's 'a part of Scotland where people just never visit';
- and, rather more seriously, that the Mull of Kintyre helicopter crash of 1993 was caused by an encounter with the jet wake of the said *Aurora* aircraft.

(All quotations from Thomas, 'Top Secret US plane "caused Chinook crash"', *The Register*, 10 July 2000.)

I should point out that these same conspiracy theorists also claim that *Aurora* travels at up to twenty times the speed of sound (the world air speed record, at the time of writing, is about eight times) and that Machrihanish's runway is over three miles long and the longest in Europe (it's actually just over two miles long and many exceed it, including some at Heathrow, for example).

Well, anyway, I tried to manoeuvre myself into a position from where I could test one of their claims. The tiptoeing didn't work and so, getting back on the bike and standing up on the pedals, I freewheeled up and down a bit until a slight rise in the ground gave me a brief glimpse of the actual runway. Was it green and yellow like the gorse that surrounded it? Was it hell... it was a fetching but unremarkable shade of runway grey of course. However, I leave the question of Machrihanish's supersecret, superstealthy, supersonic aircraft with you as an unanswered one.

The single-track road meandered up to join the main A83: right for Campbeltown, left for Glasgow (and the rest of the world). Before turning left, I peered straight ahead up Ranachan Hill, hoping to glimpse the glint of a guitar, a left-handed guitar. Alas, the steep, pastured terrain hides High Park Farm from inquisitive eyes, which is just what a young man wanted when he bought the place in the 1960s...

Macca track

High Park Farm is over a mile along a track up Ranachan Hill, and at the time of writing Paul McCartney still owns it, having bought the farm in 1966 and lived here after the whole Beatles business began to get acrimonious, saying he needed to get away from London and into the mist and mountains. He didn't quite escape all the madness, though, as it was here in Kintyre that, in order to disprove the 'Paul is dead' rumour, he was obliged to make an appearance before reporters, declaring himself 'as fit as a fiddle'.

At High Park Farm, Paul built a small recording studio in the barn (without soundproofing, being without neighbours) and here, in 1969/70, recorded the album *McCartney,* playing all instruments himself. It's understood that among the songs he wrote here were 'The Long and Winding Road' (reputedly about the B842 in East Kintyre), 'Martha My Dear' (about his sheepdog) and 'Maybe I'm Amazed', but unfortunately it's also here that he and Denny Laine penned 'Mull of Kintyre'.

The single came out in December 1977, by Christmas had sold a million and by mid-January had become the best-selling British single of all time. To millions of people around the world, all they know of Kintyre is this slushy song. As we've noted, Paul's farm isn't actually on the Mull – and the beach along which the pipers piped in the video was in fact at Saddell in East Kintyre.

As I walked my bike up a steep section of main road, the view to the south over the modern barracks of RAF Machrihanish stretched to the bulk of the Mull – more or less the same view as McCartney's higher up. The last push up to the brow, though, was rewarded by a more significant view that suddenly opened up ahead: a sensational blue swathe of ocean, with Islay squat on the horizon and, further north, a distant line of grey peaks: the Paps of Jura. This was my first glimpse of those islands that would parade their beauty across the western horizon up to and beyond Skye, and of a landscape that would accompany me all the way to Sutherland – the tantalising beauty of the deserted west coast of Scotland. Deserted, that is, except for the crowd at the first seaside lay-by: a traditional Sunday morning serving of four-by-fours, from which sprouted squeaky families heading for the beach, with a side order of bleary-eyed, droopy-drawered hippies communing around a barbecue before attacking the Atlantic surf with their boards. Next, please. A few hundred metres further on, a beach with no parking and therefore the preserve of walkers and cyclists – i.e. just me – looked a better bet for the day's first coffee break.

My map named the beach rather incongruously Port Corbert, which sounded more Cornwall than Kintyre, but this was pure Scotland. I carefully laid down the bike and, munching a Twix, wriggled a bottom shape out of the pebbles and looked back across a twinkling Machrihanish Bay to the Mull, which – it has to be said – gains in scenic attraction the further you are away from it. After luxuriating in the sun and the scene for a few minutes, I crunched my way down to the water's edge – clear as mineral water, cold as ice – and looked over to Islay, which filled the north-west horizon about 25 miles away. From most of Great Britain's coastline the sea view is uninterrupted and visions of a distant France or Holland or Ireland swim around your imagination, but out here the next land is almost always in sight, tempting you with an unplanned island hop. No time for such temptations this time, though. I'd thirty-odd miles still to get under my tyres today and so, hoisting the bike off Port Corbert's pebbles, I pointed north and set off again.

So good did it feel to be in such a place on such a day with the prospect of such pleasures to come that, as I pedalled along, I made up this little ditty:

I'm awaaaa the noooo
For this is what I doooo.
I ride up the glens
And I pass 'tween the bens
To admirrrrrre the vieoooo.

(Lucky for you there's no 'Press here to listen' button.)

Making a mental note to find out what 'the noo' actually means, I braced myself against the rare passage of a coach. Though a double-track road, the A83 was quieter the further north I travelled, traffic falling to about one vehicle a minute. For comparison, my occasional training for this ride was often along a similar-sized A-road in Leicestershire, where the ordinary midday traffic averaged about thirty vehicles a minute. East Kintyre had been around one in three minutes; yesterday's road to the Mull approximately nought in 120. Villages were pretty scarce too. Though the map lined them up – Killocraw, Cleongart, Glenbarr – most turned out to be not even hamlets, but vague settlements of scattered bungalows with the occasional house by the road or a slightly more substantial farmhouse a little way back.

After ten pleasant seaside miles, the first place with much else was Muasdale, which boasted several houses, a shop and two bus shelters, the seaward one of which offered me a flat place to sit for my packed lunch. After a morning of panoramic views it came as a strange relief to have something close to look at. The graffiti-free timetable told me the next bus in either direction would be the 13.01 to Campbeltown, which had left Glasgow at 9.00 and would even now (12.15) be sampling the delights of the 'Tarbert turning circle'. Below this was an advert for the local public transport organisation, which, it revealed, 'connected people to places'. Ah, so that's what transport does then.

Connecting myself to my bike, I set off again into the sunshine. With nothing else to report for a few miles but fresh air and empty fields, let me introduce you to my pedalled – and so far faithful – companion. Tetley, this is our reader. Reader, this is Tetley. Full name: Seamus O'Tetley, as I bought him from the cycling superstore 'Da Kettle On' (Decathlon). He was selected for this very trip from the Da Kettle On catalogue with the help of Slingers, my mate from the 1980s Soar Bottom Cycling Club, who pointed out that the other contenders all had twist-grip gears, which would have driven me not to Cape Wrath but to distraction. The choice of a Triban Trail 7 was also given the thumbs-up by the assistant at their local store, a young Australian called Tom, whose enthusiasm for mountain biking in these parts, however, fell on deaf ears, as this was definitely not my style. The route from the Mull to the Cape, following The Rule, of course, should take me only occasionally off-road and, via the miracle of the Internet, I'd already seen photos of most of these stretches of unsurfaced track. The first was a possibility tomorrow and I was confident that Tetley's lack of sturdy mountain-bike tread wouldn't be a problem. The big pluses that Tetley brought the long-distance cyclist were a comfy, wide, gel-filled saddle, bouncy front-fork suspension and – best of all for the creaky back, neck and wrists of a fifty-something – two vertical appendages to the handlebars that let me shift my weight around on long stretches where the terrain didn't shift it for me, like this 36-mile coastal haul up to Tarbert.

After an hour or so, I joined territory I'd crossed before, at Tayinloan. Two years previously my partner Julie and I had come up to the west coast during the spring monsoons and splashed down from Inverary in a hire car to this very spot, in expectation of a warm coffee and a bun among the steaming bustle of the Tayinloan ferry terminal, from where the jolly red-funnelled Caledonian MacBrayne vessel would whisk us to the island of Gigha, only about three miles from Kintyre at this point. Peering through the ceaseless rain, we caught sight of a red funnel bouncing its way across the Sound of Gigha towards us and followed a brown sign down towards the shore. Oddly, no terminal came into view. We parked in an empty car park. Still no terminal. We got out and, leaning into the rain, walked down to the water itself. No buildings at all except a wind-blown lavatory with rattling windows and a Perspex shelter with flapping timetables. From the neighbouring field, the glum stare of its single, sodden cow said 'This, mateys, is the ferry terminal.'

No coffee, no buns, no bustle, no people, no tickets, November. Well, March, actually. We deferred the trip to Gigha in favour of a dash back up to Tarbert for some warm sustenance.

Today Tayinloan was barely recognisable as that wind-blown outpost. The afternoon sun glinted off the Gigha ferry laid up for a few minutes at the jetty, off the windows of Tayinloan's roadside inn (whose convenience I resisted) and off the white walls of its public toilet (whose convenience I didn't). On emerging, I spotted a young lad of about six circling my bike on his own small-wheeled machine.

'Nice bike,' he said.

'Yours too,' I countered.

'Yeah,' he agreed and proved it by doing a wobbly wheelie before shooting back down the lane toward a group of caravans.

He was the first cyclist I'd seen all day, and only the fourth since setting off from Ardrossan two and a half days before. This struck me as extremely odd. All over Europe, including England, Sunday is cycling day and here I was on a glorious springtime Sunday pedalling along one of the most beautiful coast roads in the world and yet there were virtually no other cyclists to be seen. What's so different about Scotland?

For a while north of Tayinloan the seaward view was blocked as the road passed through woodland, before opening out again to reveal a larger CalMac (Caledonian MacBrayne) ferry heading west from Kennacraig to Port Ellen on Islay, a round trip of five hours. The vessel was emerging from West Loch Tarbert, beyond which lay the low, forested hills of Knapdale – my first view of tomorrow's terrain. Another fabulous beach slid by before a small, perfectly curved bay appeared, sporting a turquoise-doored boathouse presumably owned by the substantial house nuzzled on all sides by tall trees: Ronachan House. Until recently this place was run by the Church of Scotland to help people addicted to drugs or alcohol. It certainly looked a splendid place to be on a day like this, but I couldn't help wondering if, on a more typical Highland day, such an isolated place would drive you *to* drink rather than away from it.

Spurred on by the thought of the drink I'd deserve after a few more miles, I surged up a long gradient to be brought up short at the top by two simultaneously odd sights. On the left a signpost at the edge of some trees announced 'Soup Forest' (I could have sworn it came from tins), while on the right, a distant view of a very high but oddly familiar peak swung into view: Goat Fell on the Isle of Arran, which I'd left two days before. I'd come virtually full circle around Kintyre, a fact confirmed a little further on when I passed a sign to the Arran ferry at Claonaig. Not only did it feel as though I was rejoining civilisation but, passing the junction, I also realised I'd joined the northbound route through Scotland taken some years before by a fellow coastal cyclist, Nicholas Fairweather. As revealed in his *Coasting Around Scotland* (2002), he didn't quite get to the Mull of Kintyre, but he did cycle virtually the entire coast of Scotland. Fair play to him.

West Loch Tarbert repeatedly came and went on my left until it suddenly disappeared altogether and I was welcomed to my destination by a trilingual sign: Tarbert/Tairbeart/ Dookerville, the last in a shaky script. Scooting down into 'Dookerville', I was treated to a 'Hi there!' from a group of teenage girls sitting on the pavement and pulled up in the dazzling late-afternoon sun that anointed Tarbert harbour.

After a triumphal parade up and down the harbour front, featuring a visit to the renowned turning circle, I checked in at the friendly Islay Frigate Hotel, where my machine was assigned a back-room spot by the beer crates and I a front-room spot with harbour view and double bed, which is where I placed my weary legs for their well-deserved nap.

*

After a steamy bath and a change into my only other set of clothes (termed 'evening'), I emerged again onto the harbour front, still aglow in the balmy sunlight and, surprisingly for a Sunday evening, still a-bustle too.

Kintyre's second town is everything its first is not. My only other visit to Tarbert had been on that damp March day two years before, but even then the place immediately slotted into my Top 20 Places Just To Be. The low hills of Kintyre saunter down to the water's edge, the neat little harbour leads into tiny East Loch Tarbert – barely seven furlongs long, according to Groome's 1882 team – which then opens out into the crisp ripples of Loch Fyne, which sparkle past the headland and over as far as tree-covered Cowal's lowering presence in the east. Tarbert's harbour offers a sharp contrast to Campbeltown's empty basin, sheltering a busy cluster of fishing boats, several neat lines of pleasure craft and the CalMac ferry from Portavadie on the Cowal peninsula. Even though Tarbert is tiny by most people's standards, it has shops, hotels, an estate agent's and a choice of pubs. *Ward Lock's Red Guide: [...] Western Highlands* even reported a cinema among its 'distractions'... but then it also advertised 'the indispensable Mrs Beeton' and the National Provincial Bank, as my copy is the 1962 edition. That damp March afternoon, I'd needed no distracting from the sights of the harbourside itself and the same was true tonight, with local children and fishermen mixing with strolling couples, a map-hungry group from Germany, several passing Polish accents and an elegant olive-skinned lady who'd probably started her journey in Singapore. What Tarbert has, in short, is a sense of place.

What I really wanted right now, though, was a scent of plaice. And I'd espied the very spot to find it: a regular chippie right opposite the fishing smacks. An English friend of mine tells the tale of a young woman he met while in Tarbert a few years ago. She was evidently pretty, seemed quite refined and was altogether charming as they chatted for a while about life in Tarbert as a child in the 1960s.

'What did you and your friends do for amusement in such a quiet place?' my friend asked.

'Och, we'd hae a few laughs around the town,' said the woman.

'For example?'

'Well, for instance, we'd drive slowly past wee Hamish's chip shop, roll the windows down and shout "Hamish – yer chips are shite!"'

I trust she gets her kicks elsewhere now, as the chips were just fine. Not enough to sate my hunger, though, so I shunted along to the Tarbert Hotel, where I ordered some pasta from the Polish barman, sat with my pint (80 Shilling and excellent) opposite an English couple, also enjoying pastas and pints, and started reading up on the history of Tarbert in Groome's *Gazetteer*.

In Gaelic, *tar* means across and *ber* bring. *Tarbert* therefore means bring across. And the reason you'll find ten or more Tarberts in Scotland is that the thing a lot of people wanted to bring across was a boat; and the place they wanted to bring it across was an isthmus – to save all that sailing around, you see. So all the Tarberts are on isthmi (store that one for Scrabble). This one, of course, was the short stretch of land separating the two Lochs Tarbert and just preventing Kintyre from being another island.

I can see that the splendidly named Norseman King Magnus Barefoot, could save a fair few nautical miles by dragging his galley across this isthmus, as he – or, more probably, his dragsters – did in 1098. What I find harder to accept is that he followed up this feat by claiming that, since his boat had travelled all the way around Kintyre, it must be an island and therefore must be his legal possession, Scottish King Edgar having already ceded all western isles to him. Did Magnus think Edgar was daft? Maybe he was, for Kintyre did indeed become a Norse land until 1263. (More of the Norsemen later.)

Mr Tarberthotelsski approached and, surprisingly, beckoned me to the dining room; so I duly gathered up my pint and books, shared a puzzled glance with the English couple and followed him to a restaurant that was totally deserted but for one table laid for dinner. There I sat until a fully regaled chef delivered my pasta, which looked identical to those in the bar, wished me 'Bon appetit' and withdrew. Bemused, I ate and read.

Scouring my sources while savouring my sauces, I discovered that the folk of Tarbert are called 'Dookers' after the local word for guillemot, a source of food around here before they became a protected species (the birds, not the people); hence Dookerville. Surprisingly, Groome's *Gazetteer* seemed to be even less impressed by Tarbert than by Campbeltown, devoting to it barely a fifth of the text that described the latter. It noted the 1881 population as 1,629 (it's still about the same), most of the males being fishermen, for East Loch Tarbert 'is a curious and singularly safe and landlocked natural harbour'. Not entirely landlocked, surely, Francis.

I eventually re-trod my lonesome path to the bar to return my glass, shared another mystified shrug with the English couple and moved on.

Tarbert's hostelries are all lined up in a row facing the harbour. Next was the Anchor, which failed on the 'Can't see in' rule, and so I entered the Corner House where, just as I ordered a pint of John Smith's, my feet stuck to the floor.

'Sorry,' offered the barmaid in another Polish accent, releasing me with a rapid swish of the mop. 'It's the only way we keep our customers!' Poles seemed to be taking over from Aussies as the regulation British bar staff – and, unlike plenty of other Britons apparently, I've no problem with this. Migration is surely something to be encouraged, not only providing labour for jobs the locals either can't or won't do, but also releasing people from the suffocating effects of home... and adding a touch of cosmopolitan glamour to many a small town. Not that Tarbert seemed to need any more: the only other customers in the Corner House were a bunch of exuberant Swedes.

I'd earlier seen the remains of a tower looming over Harbour Street and now read that it was Tarbert Castle, built by, among others, Robert the Bruce in the 1320s. Amazing how many kings doubled as builders, ain't it? You never hear of Edward I moonlighting in the upholstery trade or how King Magnus Barefoot spent his spare time installing boilers, do you?

What's a bruce?

Q: What's the connection between Robert the Bruce and Winnie the Pooh?

A: They've got the same middle name.

But whereas we all know what a 'pooh' is – the kind of bear that Winnie was, of course – I had to admit to ignorance about the bruce that Robert was. Maybe it's an adjective. I'd heard of kings who were great, elder, younger, bold, unready… but if King Robert's main characteristic was his bruceness, I for one was none the wiser. Maybe it was a corruption and he was simply rather short with people: Robert the Brusque. Enough! To the research.

Well, the future king was born Robert Bruce at Turnberry in 1274. He wasn't plain Robert Bruce, though. He was born into a noble family up at the castle and by 1292, as the Earl of Carrick, he was one of two claimants to the vacant Scottish throne, losing out to John Balliol. Thirteen years later, with Balliol gone, Robert found himself in another two-horse race for the throne, but this time he was more decisive, simply murdering his challenger, John Comyn, to declare himself King of the Scots in 1306. Robert the Brute?

Fortunately for Robert's eventual elevation to the ranks of the 'Scottish Heroes' so loved by tea-towel makers, his time as king was full of rousing battles against those favourite enemies, the nasty imperialist English – including a victory at Bannockburn that allowed Robert subsequently to lead the nasty imperialist Scots on an invasion of Ireland. Robert the Bruiser?

No, 'Good King Robert', apparently – because yer man followed up Bannockburn with another stunning home victory at Arbroath, where he was the king in residence at the time of Scotland's Declaration of Independence in 1320. He died in 1329.

This is all very well. Defending the nation, beating the English, achieving independence – yes, yes, but how did he get the 'the'? Even after that goal in Argentina, Archie Gemmill was never Archie the Gemmill. OK, here's my theory: Robert was born Robert Bruce and died Robert Bruce. The 'the' is down to a book written about Robert later in the fourteenth century by John Barbour and called *The Bruce*. Barbour wrote this book not in English but medieval Scots. Could the definite article as a surname appendage have been common in Scots?

Last up on my brief harbourside tour was my own B&B, the Islay Frigate, but here the bar-flies had evaporated, leaving the lonesome barmaid to greet me with 'Aye, thank God yerr back – ah can close now.'

After two pints, pasta and chips, I concurred and happily retired to my wee room, where the soft lights of East Loch Tarbert dappled on heavy eyelids before you could say 'Dookerville'.

Chapter 3

Off the Beaten Track: Knapdale and Argyll

Having learned after only two days that my mood and the weather were to be irretrievably linked, I peered anxiously out of the Islay Frigate's empty breakfast room, which faced north. Thin cirrus hung high and lazy over Loch Fyne. Carefully leaning forward over the cereal table, I craned my neck westward.

'It's guid.'

'Wuergh!' I jumped, sprinkling the muesli with Frosties.

'The forecast's guid,' repeated a presence in the still empty room.

'Sorry, you made me jump,' I said, to the room.

'But cooler later,' said the Presence.

'Ah,' I managed, scanning around with reddening ears, hoping also to be cooler later. 'Good, good.'

The Presence suddenly decided to take the shape of a waitress behind the coffee pot, a position she had not, to my sleepy eyes, occupied seconds before.

'Will you be goin' far on yer baik today?' she said.

'No, just Lochgilphead or maybe up to Kilmartin,' I mumbled, expecting another 'Dinna bother, here's the postcard' response, but instead got:

'Och, tha's no' far. Yer'll be there in no time. Would yer laik the fool breakfast?'

It seemed appropriate.

Within half an hour I was away again, though not before Tarbert's street sweeper had shared his own view of the weather, evidently the hot local topic: 'No' a bad day fer a baik raid, but then yer nivver know in Kintyre: you can get all the wither you laik, all in the one day.'

*

The main road north hugs the shores of Loch Fyne, but The Rule took me back out on the Campbeltown Road and past the Church of Scotland, its sturdy clock tower reading ten minutes past nine, before turning right on the B8024. This led me past a neat, nine-hole golf course occupying the western end of the isthmus and straddling a small stream, the route along which old Magnus Barefoot would have forced his men to drag that boat from loch to loch (another 'apparently', if you ask me). Anyway, as I pedalled over the stream, I left Kintyre and entered Knapdale.

Being English, I'm used to identifying areas by their county: I might trundle up the lane into deepest Worcestershire or drive from Norfolk down into Suffolk, for example. But these Highland counties are so huge (for days my route would be entirely within the county of Argyll and Bute) that the local tendency to use bits and pieces of physical geography turns out to be a useful tool. The wriggly coastline and dramatic scenery around here make it pretty easy to identify separate chunks of land: while Kintyre was a single peninsula, Knapdale is three in one and extends from the Lochs Tarbert northwards to the Crinan Canal – and so, if things went well, would my day.

The single-track lane rose away from the lochside, leaving a triangular strand covered this April with a thick yellow carpet of flowers. The gay scene was further brightened by the crimson of a post van buzzing along the same route as me. Indeed, there was no other. It would overtake me with a cheery parp, only to stop at the next cottage, where the tireless postman would leap out to deliver his bundle of letters and a merry quip while I would overtake him in turn. This little dance went through several rounds before we entered a patch of thick, steep woodland where, as I progressed steadily on foot, Postman Parp chugged off into the distance. He was to be the last human I saw for about an hour.

The woods I'd entered comprised first ancient oaks and then less ancient conifers, many of which had already been felled. This was all Knapdale Forest, but the lochside stretch I was rolling through formed the trickily named Achaglachgach Forest, where I panted up and down Glen

Achaglachgach, past Achaglachgach House and through Achaglachgach village, which was totally deserted. Maybe they'd all choked to death trying to say 'Achaglachgach'.

After Dunmore (easier on the throat, but still empty), the road turned inland and a few clearings began to appear, from one of which a herd of deer scuttled away as my tyres crunched into their world. I'd now left the banks of West Loch Tarbert and was heading over to my first new loch of the day: little Loch Stornoway. Unusually, the road doesn't hug the shores of the loch, but skirts the meadows at its head, where a convenient gate invited me to pull up for a chocolate break and a stare at the standing stones and sheep, some of which dozed under the stones, while others baaed.

Nobody seems sure of the significance of these two prehistoric stones, one about the height of two men, the other rather shorter, but the fact that they lie almost exactly on a north–south line suggests that they may have been raised after either observing the shadow of the midday sun or locating the celestial north pole in the night sky.

As I broke off a last chunk of chocolate, the baaing intensified and I spotted a human head bobbing up and down behind a hedge to the right of the stones. As I packed up my bits and pieces, he bobbed into full view and waved. As I waved back and picked up my bike, he bobbed into a trot, still waving, and so I delayed mounting up.

'No' a bad mornin',' he panted from a few metres away.

After the usual opening forays on the day's forecast, we fell into conversation. He was the farmer here and his sheep were baaing in expectation of food, but as usual, he said, they'd got the time of day wrong and he was merely doing his morning casualty tour – none today. Politely declining an invitation to take a closer look at 'his' stones, I pushed off as he waved me on my way. It soon dawned on me that while I'd seen no other human for an hour, he'd probably seen none since dawn.

As the route climbed the steepening north shore of Loch Stornoway, a view of nearby islands opened up to my left. As always, the immediate task was to figure out which ones they were: still Gigha and its offshoots, my handlebar map told me. Rounding a sharp bend, I was suddenly surrounded by a powerful scent and then, turning the next, by the gorse bushes that had released it into the light westerly breeze. They rose either side of a steep stretch of tarmac that I climbed on foot until, at the brow of the hill, all undergrowth fell away to reveal the broad grey swathe of the Sound of Jura, beyond which lay another new view: not only the Paps but all of Jura's misty peaks strung out like the teeth of an upturned, sunken saw.

Just like the previous day, Jura was to hold fast on my left for miles and miles while the road ducked and dived through countless diverse, smaller-scale landscapes. The next one was unusual, although I knew it was coming: a pub. Yes, here in the middle of Knapdale's wild circuit was a renowned hostelry that boasted not only good food and comfy rooms but also something about which I'd been fantasising all morning: a cup of real coffee.

Accelerating into Kilberry, I swerved to my right and came to a triumphant halt in front of the Kilberry Inn. Which was closed. Closed Monday lunchtimes. So, it appeared, was Kilberry itself. Opposite the tasteful inn stood a tasteless caravan on which its occupants had scrawled, in garish colours and juvenile script: 'Explore. Interact. Enjoy. Places to Visit. People to Annoy.'

Well, treating 'enjoy' as an intransitive verb certainly does it with me. Pleased at least that Kilberry's witless hippies were absent or still asleep, I pedalled onward, due north.

Being on another human-free stretch, I began to ponder the area's emptiness. Guidebooks are fond of calling Knapdale 'remote' or 'off the beaten track', but the odd thing was that, despite the evident lack of humanity, it didn't feel actually remote to me at all – certainly less so than the Mull of Kintyre. I think we travellers could benefit from a spot of scientific rigour in our reckless descriptions of remoteness.

Are you really somewhere remote? Here's my proposal for figuring out your own answer to that question.

Start off with ten points and then lose one each time you answer 'Yes' to one of the following questions:

- Could you walk to somewhere that sells hot food by the next mealtime?
- Can you see a surfaced road?
- If you can, would you bother to look both ways before crossing it?
- Does any form of public transport pass here at least once a week? (Vapour trails don't count.)

- Can you hear people talking about the same subjects that you do? (Travelling companions don't count.)
- Is the nearest real coffee less than five miles away as the coffee bean flies?
- Can you hear any non-natural sounds? (Elvis Costello on your iPod doesn't count.)
- Are you confident that the newspaper you'd buy at the nearest newsagent is today's?
- Do you see any locals with mobile phones?
- If you collapsed from exhaustion, or indeed from extreme remotitis (see under R = 5 below), would the emergency vehicle that picks you up arrive by land?

(Feel free to add questions more relevant to your nationality of choice. For example, Australians may want to replace real coffee with cold beer; the Dutch may want to replace the sound from an iPod with the sound of chocolate sprinkles.)

If you can't come up with a single 'Yes', and therefore remain on ten points, you're in an Officially Remote Location. And I hope you've got a view, a sleeping bag and a week's supply of Marmite. If your score sinks to zero, stop – you're in Covent Garden. And no, popping round the corner to Stanford's still won't make a difference.

Using the above system, I have developed my own Scale of Remoteness, which I present to you here...

Guise's Scale of Remoteness

R=	Description	Key Features
0	Home	You can drift in and out of sleep with no one noticing.
1	Round the corner	Slippers are still OK.
2	Down the road	You see someone you don't know.
3	Over there	You might take a different route home.
4	Away	The nearest newsagent may not stock *The New Statesman*.
5	In the sticks	Signs of remotitis become evident among the local population, e.g. staring at strangers or talking to trees.
6	Far away	The nearest newsagent has not heard of *The New Statesman*.
7	Off the beaten track	Signs of remotitis are rife among the local population.
8	Up shit creek	You develop remotitis and wonder how long it will be before your bones are discovered.
9	Way out yonder	You discover someone's bones.
10	Officially remote	Bones? You mean another human has actually passed this way?

By this test and scale, as I trundled up the west coast of Knapdale, R was 7 and I was merely 'off the beaten track' and so some of the guidebooks were right. Mind you, this depended on my wrong guess of 'Yes' to the coffee question. A retrospective calculation for the start of this journey made R for the Mull to be 8 ('up shit creek').

The wind had now strengthened and was blowing from the south, which was good for my progress but tricky for finding somewhere to have my packed lunch, until I spotted a north-facing drystone wall at the entrance to a farm track opposite the mouth of Loch Caolisport. Once again my break coincided with a rare human appearance, this time more obviously a farmer as he emerged from a sheep field astride his quad bike, with a sheepdog perched precariously on the back and a memorable nose/moustache combination perched dramatically on his face.

He too seemed glad of some company. He'd been farming here for only a few years, having moved up from the Lowlands. No, he didn't tire of the views from his land, as the weather constantly changed their character, and yes, there'd been some spectacular sunsets these last few days and, well, he was sorry that Jura had now decided to hide behind the mist just as a visitor was passing. Assuring him I didn't hold him personally responsible, I mentioned the farmer I'd met back at Loch Stornoway. Farmer Moustache knew him well.

'Did you get the tour of his standing stones?'

'No, I just looked at them from the road.'

'Oh dear, he's quite proud of them.'

Oh dear.

All the while his master was talking, the dog sat calmly on the quad bike, its back to us and its eyes fixed on the grazing sheep beyond the gate. Even as I gathered up my things and Farmer Moustache waved me off with a warning about the coming rain, his canine companion never took its eyes off the field.

The further I cycled along the low pebbly shore of Loch Caolisport, the more I realised I'd rejoined the beaten track. First a car or two, then pedestrians that didn't want to stop and talk, then a post van that didn't parp, then a bin lorry and finally, heralded by the sounds of what we used to call 'Music and Movement', a little blue school with little children bouncing around a little blue playground.

This was Achahoish and I knew it was decision time. There were two possible routes from here to the north. Plan A was to stick to the west coast: carry on around the head of the loch through (yes) Lochead and along the opposite shore until, according to my map, the surfaced lane would run out at Ellary, from where an unsurfaced track would rear up and, after pointing me perilously at the rugged Point of Knap, throw me a surfaced lifeline down into the hamlet of Kilmory and along beautiful Loch Sween until eventually disgorging me by the Crinan Canal at Bellanoch. Plan B (permitted under The Rule's 'viability' clause by the advanced hour and the lack of booked accommodation) was to take a short cut and follow the B8024 to rejoin Loch Fyne a few miles north of Tarbert, where I'd turn northwards with the wind at my back and a hot bath on my mind.

It was already after two, the talk was of rain and my snap had run out. This, I believe, is what Americans mean by a 'no brainer'. Plan B.

My disappointment that I'd already used the 'viability' clause to skip a section of Knapdale's beautiful west coast was tempered by a realisation of the challenge ahead. Only a few metres out of Achahoish I got out of one saddle to start the long haul over another: that which separated Knapdale's first peninsula from its second. The crucial number on my map was 193: the spot height in metres at the top of the pass. While I'm bilingual with distances and weights, for some reason I've never got my head around metric heights, even my own – I know I'm five foot six, but could be just as easily one metre, ten metres or a hundred metres tall, for all I know. This had begun to change in the last three days. From the moment I'd puffed up to the 199-metre dot between the east and west coasts of Arran en route to Kintyre to start this ride, I knew that a 200-metre climb from sea level was something your legs would remember. Here was another. It took forty minutes to trudge the two miles through the evergreens up to Loch Arail and precisely nine minutes to whizz the same distance down the other side to the banks of Loch Fyne. Clock-watching is an occupational obsession for the lone cyclist.

The A83 by Loch Fyne and Loch Gilp is *not* a recommended cycling route: holiday coaches and Tesco lorries yes, bikes no. After about thirty miles on a lonesome trail it was odd to be suddenly sharing my route with so many and such huge vehicles. Maybe the more natural hazards of a late finish on Plan A would have been better after all. I focused on safety. According to a report by the *Science Journal* that I'd read about in *The Times*, cycling 650 miles (the approximate length of this journey) was exposing me to the same risk of death as driving 10,000 miles by car or paddling for seven hours by canoe; or drinking 44 bottles of wine or eating 2,700 tablespoons of peanut butter. Doing either of the last two just before any of the first three probably more than doubles the risk, I'd say.

Confident of finding somewhere to stay at Lochgilphead, I pulled into Ardrishaig for a temporary respite from the buffets and fumes.

For some canals – Panama, Suez – the rationale is obvious; for others, less so. The Crinan Canal falls squarely in the Panama camp: you can sail the 120 miles around Kintyre, negotiating a notorious accident black spot on your way past the Mull, or you can be towed or chugged through a flooded nine-mile trench from Ardrishaig to Crinan. So thought John Rennie who started to build the canal (with some help, I would guess) in 1794, finishing in 1801. Its first customers were mostly fishing vessels, but they were joined later by passenger boats, including some paddle steamers of the company that eventually became Caledonian MacBrayne, benefiting from the shorter route between Glasgow and the West Highlands and Islands. The later opening of the Caledonian Canal further north meant that some shipping from Glasgow could even pass this way en route to the North Sea at Inverness.

Because of the low waters further north at the head of Loch Gilp, Ardrishaig became the eastern terminus of the Crinan Canal and its route through the back streets of this small town still defines the place. I pedalled beside it, past the first two locks and over one of the small bridges. As I leant against the parapet, a slightly overweight, middle-aged man laden with shopping panted up to me. Knowing by now the rarity of cyclists around these parts, I had my answers at the ready:

'From the Mull of Kintyre to Cape Wrath.'

'Don't know – I'll add up the miles when I've finished.'

'No, no charity. Just for fun.'

This local seemed more interested in me than the weather.

'Och, I used to raid a baik. Hark a' me! Used to? I've still got it in the shed. How old are you, son?'

I told him.

'Wha'! Yui're older'n me!'

'Maybe you should get your bike out of the shed again.' It was the obvious suggestion, but it seemed to hit him like a ray of sunshine on a dark winter's afternoon.

'Am awa' there noo! Cape Wrath, you say? Aye, it's possible.' Gathering up his burden of toilet rolls and Domestos, he added, 'Good luck, son… fella, I mean!'

I made a mental note to look out for him at the Cape.

★

Groome's *Gazetteer* marks Lochgilphead down as 'a prosperous and well-built town' of 1,489 souls, featuring five good inns, a 'mutual improvement association' and the Argyll and Bute District Asylum for the Insane, erected twenty years before by the Lunacy Board.

Today's Lochgilphead, now the administrative centre of the whole of Argyll and Bute, has swollen to about 3,000 souls, though I can't say how many are insane or how many need improving. What I can say is that, with the weather closing in that late Monday afternoon and its residents scurrying around with their collars turned up, the town itself seemed to hunch its grey shoulders to keep me out as I approached. It's at the head of the loch in name only, for Loch Gilp hereabouts is all mud and mush: good news for wading birds perhaps, but bad news for the townscape. There was just something about the place that didn't appeal to me — maybe it was because it's a planned town, maybe the main street was too wide, maybe the open water was too far away. In any case, by the time I'd found the tourist information centre, I'd decided not to stay.

I asked for a list of guest houses in Kilmartin, ten miles or so up the road.

'We don't have any registered there, I'm afraid, sir.'

'I don't mind whether they're registered, I'd just like a list.'

'Sorry, sir, we don't have one. Of course, there may be some *private* hotels up there.'

What other kind of hotels are there? State-run, communist bunk-houses? I thanked her and left. Anyway, I'd got a list in my saddlebag but was just too lazy to get it out. So I joined the hectic northbound A816, distracting myself from the proximity of the trucks by looking out for the canal route out to the west. Wait a minute! Canals mean towpaths and towpaths mean flat, quiet cycling. Idiot! At Cairnbaan I eschewed the diesel delights of the main road to join the towpath for a pleasant mile or two as far as Bellanoch, where the canal and I diverged as I headed out along a single-track road across Mòine Mhòr ('the big bog').

I was entering a tract of terrain crucial to the history not just of Argyll but of Scotland. Kilmartin Glen, the stretch of country between the Crinan Canal and Kilmartin, including Mòine Mhòr as its southern part, seems to have been peculiarly popular with our distant ancestors. Within six miles of Kilmartin there are no less than 150 prehistoric monuments of one kind or another: not only standing stones, burial cairns and rock carvings from the New Stone Age, but also the mysterious 'cup and ring' markings from the Bronze Age. Each of these comprises a round hollow surrounded by a number of concentric rings and the reason they're usually described as 'mysterious' is that no one seems to have a convincing explanation of what on earth they were used for.

In other circumstances it would have been fun to wander from the road to investigate some of the sites scattered all over the map, but by now my body was feeling very much like a prehistoric site itself, the clouds were doing everything rainlike except actually dropping their burden and my sights were set firmly along the dart-straight road on the comforts of a bed in Kilmartin. Through the gathering dusk, though, I could just make out a dark hillock rising dramatically from the bog to the east: the site of fortifications from a later age.

This is the heart of Argyll – the coast of the Gaels – as it's here that these invaders from Ireland also set up their capital, on that very hillock: the sixth-century fort of Dunadd, royal palace of the old kingdom of Dalriada. This is thought to have been the original location for the 'Stone of Destiny' used in Scottish coronations (and, after being stolen by the English, in British coronations). Within the fort is still to be found a foot-shaped depression, supposedly made by the foot of Fergus, first king of Dalriada, and into which each successive king would place his own foot as part of his installation ceremony. The Scots seem to have a thing about footprints: no doubt I wouldn't have been able to find that one either.

By the time I'd rejoined the main road, both the sky and the landscape had turned the colour of black pudding, with the lights of Kilmartin just punching through in the distance. The last hundred metres was another bike-walk and, just as I realised the lights came almost entirely from the Kilmartin Hotel, giant raindrops at last began to fall. Rushing my machine around the back of the inn and under a convenient parasol, I burst into the welcoming glow of the main bar, a sweaty, yellow-black infidel in a cool temple of tartan.

A late cancellation had freed up a room just for me. With special permission, I shouldered the muddy machine into the bedroom itself where it served as an emergency clothes horse as I clambered into the shower before collapsing onto a bed big enough for three. Earlier that day I may have missed the Point of Knap but would never miss the point of nap and so descended into a long and heavy one.

★

No pub crawls tonight, I thought an hour later as I perched myself on a stool at the only bar in town. After a pint and a perusal of the menu, I popped out into the porch to make a phone call just as three racing bikes swished by in the overdue rain, which was certainly making up for lost time. They were the only other cyclists I'd seen all day.

Soon after I'd settled at the bar again, the door opened and in blew a small, grey-haired man of about sixty in a tweed jacket glistening with fresh raindrops. When he sat down at the bar he was taller. The landlord immediately dropped what he was doing to greet the newcomer.

'Is it congratulations, Hamish?'

'Aye, it is. It's a boy!' declared Hamish in triumph.

'Hurrah!' cheered all three bar staff in unison.

'Mother and babby are doin' fain.'

'Hurrah!'

'And his name is Camron, with no "e".'

'Hur…. wha'?'

'Am jus' tellin' yous wha' oor Alec jus' told me. It's C-a-m-r-o-n.'

'But Cameron's got an "e". Even tha' David Cameron's got an "e".'

'Well,' muttered Hamish, his triumph slightly punctured, 'this one's a Cam-Ron and dinna blame me – I had nothin' tae do wi' it.'

'Och well, Hamish, a dram on the house all the same?'

'Och, whae no'? Cheers!'

'Cheers!' chorused all at the bar, including me – now realising that Alec was the baby's father and Hamish the triumphant grandfather. He returned my raised glass.

Two younger men soon entered and greeted Hamish with more congratulations, more queries on the name and another dram. To cut a long evening short, every new customer got the same tale and raised the same glasses. Hamish's views on the issue of the missing 'e' sank from puzzlement through melancholy to distress:

'Ma wee boy's goin' to grow up wi' no "e"… What kind o' start in life is tha'?'

By the time I'd been to dinner and back, two middle-aged women were sitting either side of Hamish, one with an old-fashioned headscarf propped halfway up her head. 'Doon the road,' whispered Mrs MacScarf, 'I've seen a car wi' CAM 99 as the number. You could buy the lad that as a christening gift!'

Hamish was not to be cheered up.

'Aye,' opined her friend, 'and the village needs more young boys. There's – wha'? – only faiv or sex at the school. Which lass'll young Cam-Ron be right fer? Young Katie MacWilliam's wee girrrl mus' be aboo' two – that'll be the one for yuir lad, Hamish.'

'The boy's no' but a few hours old,' complained Hamish loudly, 'and you've already go' the puir wee lad set up wi' a car and now a bloody waif!' The whole bar laughed out loud and I left them to it, giggling my way upstairs.

Over dinner I'd measured my day at 46 miles: hardly Tour de France standard, but my longest day yet. When the Presence at breakfast had predicted that I'd 'be there in no time', she was doubtless thinking of the direct route, not the tour around Knapdale's outer reaches. By whichever way, I was pleased to have made it to the Big Bed by the Big Bog and, with a weary sigh, gave it the Big Nod.

Chapter 4

A Hard Rain:
Argyll and Lorn

Mòine Mhòr, the big bog so popular with our ancestors, is even today a magnet for another class of *Homo sapiens*: ecologists in general and bog fans in particular. I can't say that I've come across many bog fans myself, but any doubts as to their existence were dismissed by a notice outside Kilmartin Museum announcing a talk to be given two days later: 'Mosses, Lichens and Spongiforms' by the splendidly named Peter Quelch. As I'm sure Mr Quelch would tell you, Mòine Mhòr is the biggest raised bog in Western Scotland. I wonder why some of us find such things slightly hilarious? Maybe it's just me.

I'd come over to the museum before breakfast, before the day's rains started, to take a look at the medieval grave slabs in the churchyard next door. Everything was washed clean from the night's storms and glistened in the rays of the misty sun that struggled up the sky above the glen to the south, casting deep shadows across the relief of the slabs. They date from the 1300s to the 1700s and their designs were not only intricate, with metre-long interwoven carvings, but also crystal clear: here a farm implement ready for use, there a sword looking as sharp as the day it was made, here a sheaf of wheat, there a coat of arms. The collection – the biggest in Western Scotland – kept me occupied until the day's first raindrops sent me back to the hotel in search of breakfast.

With everywhere so quiet and peaceful I thought I was the only one up and about, but as I crossed the road back to the hotel a small figure, crumpled around the collar and grey around the gills, scurried along to the northbound bus stop. It was Hamish, no doubt away to the hospital to admire his new grandson, e-less or not. I waved but he didn't see me.

About forty-five minutes after a hungry human re-entered the Kilmartin Hotel's back door, there emerged into the grey day a fully-togged, luminous yellow alien. I may have looked daft, but, finally following the Third Law of Cycle Touring, at least I now knew my kit.

As I squelched and swooshed past the museum, which, alas, wouldn't be opening for over an hour, I kept a lookout for its curator in case he was still scratching. A few years

before, this man – brave or batty, take your pick – had sat
semi-naked one summer evening in a local spot renowned
for its midges, on a mission to raise money for his museum
from every midge bite he received. He raised a substantial
sum. I hope it's not in the next curator's job description.

The meddlesome mite

The tiny thing is called *culicoides impunctatus* and it gets only
a tiny mention – if any at all – in most guidebooks to the
Highlands, but if you're in the wrong place at the wrong
time it's the biggest memory you take away.

The Highland midge is smaller than the mosquito but,
then again, it appears in larger numbers. Its bite is smaller
than the mosquito's but, then again, it itches just as much. It's
the female that bites, as she can lay eggs only after feasting on
blood – your blood.

Midges like damp areas, low sunlight, no wind and dark
clothes (to land on, not to wear). So your best bet for a
midge-free summer highland holiday is to don a white robe
and take a packet of porridge to, say, Ethiopia at midday.
Alternatively, you could simply avoid the summer, which is
exactly what I'd done: the midge season is variously said to
start in May or June and last until August or September. Oh,
and they don't like the east coast of Scotland, by the way.
Or England. They must be a bloody nuisance at the travel
agent's.

Other than not coming in summer, there are two other ways
to avoid getting bitten. You could use one of many insect
repellents, of which the most frequently recommended to
me is 'Skin So Soft' by Avon – not designed for the purpose,
but allegedly effective. You could wear a midge hood, which
makes you look like a beekeeper and makes eating, drinking

and passing through doorways a challenge. The best home-made midge hood I've seen was a pile of tea towels around the head of the Salen Inn's owner one still June evening on Ardnamurchan, when my own problems with the beasts prompted the following verse.

MACMIDGE

The tedious thing about midges
Is midges are tedious things.
Like the women of France,
They are straight in your pants.
If I was God I would cut off their wings.
The midge world is centred on Scotland,
Where they focus their airborne attacks –
Not on the locals,
Those lucky old yokels,
But on innocent, wee Sassenachs.
The next time I'm north of the border
I'll go full prepared for the fight.
With a crate full of spray
And bazooka I may
Just defeat the meddlesome mite.

(By the author, with assistance from Julie and apologies to Tigger)

Today's midge-free, springtime stint was to be just a short, 28-mile lurch directly to Oban – do not pass GO, do not collect £200 – which may well have been a gloriously scenic route on another day, but on this torrential Tuesday and without my spectacles (splattered to the point of blindness within a minute), it was just, I have to say, rather dreary. Which is why I'm going to spare you the splash-by-splash commentary.

Suffice to say that, thanks to my myopic eyes, I found interest only in the poetry of the regular signposts: Carnassarie, Lunga, Barravullin; Lochs Craignish, Melfort and Feochan; Kils -martin, -melford and -ninver. Plus Arduaine, where, naturally, the 'ard rain was still a-fallin'. Most place names in these parts are poor anglicisations of the even more poetic Gaelic. 'Kil' is an anglicisation of *'cill'*, a church; 'Inver' an anglicisation of *'inbhir'*, a meeting of rivers. In fact, here's a useful little list, from which you can figure out your own translations.

> **Some clues to Gaelic place names (anglicisations in brackets)**
>
> *ach* = field
> *achlaise* = armpit
> *am* = the
> *àrd* = high
> *bà* = cattle
> *baile* (balla) = farm, hamlet
> *beag* (beg) = little
> *bealach* = pass
> *beinn* (ben) = peak
> *camas* = bay
> *caol* (kyle) = narrow or narrows
> *ceann* (kin) = headland
> *cill* (kil) = church
> *còinneach* = moss
> *dubh* = black
> *dùn* = fortress

eilean (ellan) = island
geal = white
ghobhar = goat
inbhir (inver) = meeting of rivers
innis (inch) = island
mòr = big
rubha = headland
sgùrr = rocky peak
srath (strath) = valley
taigh = house

So if you want to discourage Gaelic-speaking visitors, you might name your house *'Taighachlaise'*.

None of the signposts, however, gave me as much food for thought as the one near the head of Loch Craignish, which announced 'Oven-Ready Geese'. What could have convinced its writer of this state? Perhaps a conversation with the geese along these lines...

'OK, geese, are you ready for the oven?'

'Well, actually, we'd just like to finish this crossword in *Goose Gazette* first.'

'Fifteen minutes?'

'It's the cryptic one.'

'Show me. Hm. One across: Ideal state for a goose, rhymes with toast, five letters. Cryptic?'

'OK, we'll be ready in fifteen minutes.'

The wet water of the west was evidently seeping through my cranium.

At the first coffee stop, in a bus shelter near Garraron, my map told me not only that the misty islands hovering just across the water were Shuna, Luing and Scarba, but also that I'd slipped into another area. From the Crinan Canal northwards I'd been edging out of the traditional area of Argyll across its western lip (even though, confusingly, I was still well inside the modern county of Argyll and Bute), and somewhere here around the head of Loch Craignish I'd entered Lorn. The district of Lorn is named after the tribe of Loarn, which in turn is thought to have been named after Loarn, brother of King Fergus, he of the footprint at Dunadd, and extends from Loch Craignish in the south to Loch Leven about forty miles to the north.

Saddled up again, I could see even without specs that, whether it was in Argyll or Lorn, the misty terrain was still sparsely populated and the traffic that splashed past, though heavier than the previous two days, was still only about one vehicle every few minutes. And so it came as rather a shock when, after about five hours of continuous nothing, I slithered down another hill, rounded another corner and suddenly found myself pedalling into a proper town – with proper traffic, proper traffic jams, proper traffic lights (first in five days) and even a proper traffic warden. This was Oban – or, to use what seems to be its full name, Obangatewaytotheisles. It was to be the end of the first stage of this journey.

Obangatewaytotheisles is a relatively young town: even the fishing village around which it developed is barely 200 years old. In the 1791 *Statistical Accounts of Scotland* there's no entry for Oban at all; by 1843 it had sneaked in, though only as part of the parish of Kilmore and Kilbride, with one hotel and 'a number of public houses, some of which afford too many facilities for indulging in the use of ardent spirits'.

(Various, *The Statistical Accounts of Scotland*.) By 1882 Oban's population had grown to 3,896 and now it's about 8,500, making it the second biggest town on Scotland's west coast and the biggest on this journey.

Two main factors explain its growth in the nineteenth century. First, its location on the fine natural harbour of Oban Bay, with deep moorings sheltered by the island of Kerrera, barely a mile offshore, led to its being chosen as the west-coast hub of the ferry operations that were to become Caledonian MacBrayne. The 'MacBrayne' in the name came from David MacBrayne, one of the original partners in the 1851 firm; 'Caledonian' from the later inclusion of the Caledonian Steam Packet Company. The company is now owned by the Scottish Executive and one oddity is that almost every one of its ferries is named after a place that a ferry does *not* serve. Nowadays, for many regular visitors to the Isles their first glimpse of a red-funnelled 'CalMac' ferry must be the signal that they've arrived.

Second, there came the railway. Oban is the first of three rail termini I would pass en route north, each at the western end of a magnificent branch line piercing the inhospitable terrain of Scotland's north-west coast. The Callander and Oban Railway Company's line reached Oban in 1880, giving rail access to Glasgow, Edinburgh and beyond and opening the town up to the burgeoning Victorian holiday trade. The original terminal building, which Groome's *Gazetteer* called 'one of the prettiest and most graceful buildings of the town' was, alas and alack, demolished in 1985 and its replacement is, like the new ferry terminal alongside, a sad and unimaginative rectangular block that does its best to destroy the glorious setting. However, the fact that this line still survives in the vulnerable, privatised world of twenty-first-century public transport is one worth celebrating.

When Groome's team visited Oban in the early 1880s, the tourist boom following the railway's arrival was in full swing; this may explain in part the evident enthusiasm in this extract:

> When the tourist season once begins, Oban is bustling and gay. Train and steamer and coach pour streams of eager pleasureseekers into the town – all countries of the world are represented, all ages and ranks in its hotels and streets. The shriek of the engines, the clear tones of the steamerbells, and the rumble of wheels are heard more frequently; the hotels hoist their flags; bands play on the promenade; graceful white-sailed yachts glide into the bay and drop anchor; tourists and canvas-shoed yachtsmen throng the streets and shops; and there is a general air of bustle and of coming and going. (*Ordnance Gazetteer of Scotland*, 1882)

I find it hard to believe that *all* countries of the world were represented. I heard no bands myself and shirked from any close examination of sailors' footwear, but otherwise Obangatewaytotheisles seemed pretty much as observed 125 years before.

I've a strange family connection with the town. Quite late in life, my mother's sister married a Scotsman she'd met at the office where they both worked in Slough. As a teenager

I was fascinated by Uncle Frank, though a little in awe of him too. He spoke with a heavy Scots brogue, wore a pair of them too, smoked a heavy brown pipe and possessed several heavy bookcases chock-full of heavy tomes on heavy subjects, including Scottish history. In every one of these regards, he was unique in our family. He was from Oban, my aunt had told us, and I would ask him about his home there, his work, where he was born, his family. Whatever the question, Uncle Frank would always give the same answer: 'Aye, Oban. A fine place indeed.'

We never met any of his family until he died, shortly after my aunt, in the 1980s. At the funeral in Derbyshire, where they'd lived after retiring, I spoke to a few of Frank's family before the service and noted that none had a Scottish accent. In the vicar's summary of his life, some news caused an audible intake of breath from one half of the congregation: 'Frank was a quiet man who, when taking up a post in Scotland, took so well to his new home that he adopted its ways and manners, eventually giving the impression to new acquaintances that he hailed from there. Frank was born and bred in Shropshire.'

Good old Uncle Frank.

The rain had finally dripped to a sort of stop and so, soon after sloshing into town, I gravitated to the Esplanade and there feasted my newly respectacled eyes on a scene that Uncle Frank must have watched many a time: the constant coming and going of the CalMac ferries across Oban Bay – before feasting my tum on a late lunch of piping-hot leek and potato soup at a convenient cafe on George Street. The warm bowl also thawed out my thumbs, numbed from the combination of damp Atlantic air and the frantic gear-switching that was already a defining feature of this trip.

I'm always impressed by those travellers who, in these hectic times, still follow the fictional lead of Phileas Fogg and launch into their journey with no intention of returning home until the job is complete. Who looks after Simon Reeve's home while he's circumnavigating the globe? Who opens Bill Bryson's mail? Mows their lawns? An ideal world would have seen me charge straight from the Mull to the Cape, but my little world, like many, is not ideal and this jaunt would have to be done in three stages.

Stage 1 ended right there in the steaming Oban cafe. The Highlands had already treated me to some serious exercise, some sharp lessons and rather more rain-free hours than I'd a right to expect. More importantly, they'd heightened my eagerness to see more of this unique and rewarding region, just as soon as I could get foot to pedal again.

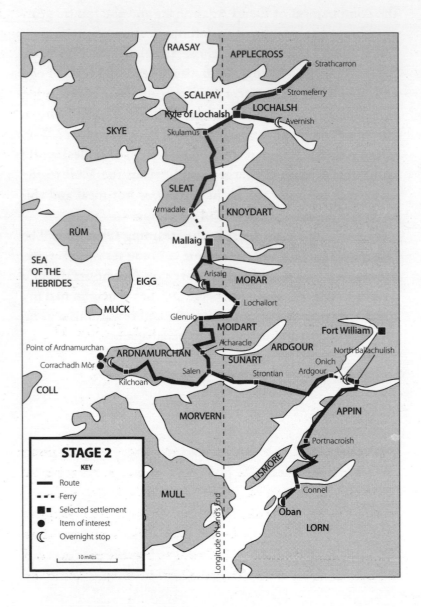

STAGE 2

KEY

— Route
- - - Ferry
■ ■ Selected settlement
● Item of interest
☾ Overnight stop

10 miles

Chapter 5

Another Murrrrder or Two: Lorn, Benderloch, Appin and Lochaber

While the summer midges had come and (I hoped) gone from the Highlands, I'd gone and come, resurfacing at Oban railway station one Tuesday evening in September – with Tetley in tow again, of course. My train from Glasgow squeaked into Oban just before four o'clock and so, after checking in at Mrs Mac's, I had time to breathe in some cool Atlantic air again, after another record-breaking summer of sweat south of the border, and to take a personal look at one Oban edifice I'd not had time to see last spring.

A watery sun squinted down on the healthy green lawns of the Esplanade as I sauntered along, taking in once again the sights and sounds of the bay: the small CalMac ferry that serves the island of Lismore drifted around the point of Kerrera's low hills and past the monument to David Hutcheson, founder of the ferry operations; a green fishing smack chugged out in the opposite direction; a white-sailed yacht hung about indecisively near Kerrera's shore; and a skitter of tiny, unidentifiable birds skipped among the wavelets on Oban's narrow beach, drawing the pointing fingers of children being manoeuvred along by their harassed parents. Groome's 'general air of bustle' was alive and well.

At the square I crossed George Street to turn up Argyll Street, a route I knew would take me to a building that I'd seen from afar but never visited, a structure that seems to have provoked extreme – and extremely opposite – reactions ever since it was built, which unfortunately was just too late for our man Groome to pass down his valued judgement on it. I girded my loins for the climb up to McCaig's Tower.

In the 1890s John Stewart McCaig was a local banker with money on his hands in a town where most of the stonemasons had time on theirs. To give them some employment and to make a mark on his home town, McCaig set up a project to build a vast structure housing both museum and art gallery. Unfortunately, McCaig died in 1897 and the building work was abandoned. What remains is an enormous circular wall of granite, matching approximately the general layout of Rome's Colosseum (which McCaig had visited) and dubbed

'McCaig's Folly' – which seems a little harsh as he surely didn't intend to die just then.

Opinion, as I said, has been divided. A recent guidebook calls it 'incongruous' (Alan Murphy, *Footprint Travel Guide: Scotland Highlands and Islands Handbook*); an earlier one saw 'a vast and conspicuous folly' (*Ward Lock's Red Guide: [...] Western Highlands*); while Lister believed it added 'a pleasant touch of fantasy to the Victorian scene' (John Lister, *The Scottish Highlands*).

At the end of Argyll Street, the stone steps of Jacob's Ladder took me into a rather dilapidated area of town, half-buried in weeds and infused with the stale, back-bar smell from a nearby distillery. Eventually, however, I emerged on a narrow lane with genteel cottages and followed the signs to the tower. In the gloaming, the approach to the structure was rather dark and eerie, its walls looming even higher than I'd expected. Way above the main entrance I could just make out an inscription that declared McCaig to be not just a banker, but 'Art Critic and Philosophical Essayist' too. Inside, though, the setting sun flooded the neatly grassed slopes with a golden light and the views through and beyond the wall's regular openings were magnificent, taking in the isles of Kerrera, Mull and Lismore and the distant purple mountains of Morvern, as well as the ever-busy bay and town of Oban itself.

Take your pick from the above opinions on McCaig's Tower, but I'm with Lister's 'touch of fantasy'. It's free to visit too.

After a knee-throbbing descent back to the Esplanade, I descended still further: into the downstairs bar of the

Oban Inn for a perusal of my next day's route over a pint of 80 Shilling. The bar was packed but, save for the barman, not a Scottish accent was to be heard, tonight's dominant tones being German, American and English. The same was true when I popped into the next pub along, where I had the misfortune to sit next to the one customer looking for a conversational victim. He was from Manchester and, with neither invitation nor encouragement, revealed to me several unrelated facts: that England's disputed 1966 World Cup goal had been proven to have crossed the line 'by differentiation'; that the recent discovery of three 'planetoids' of the same classification as Pluto was all nonsense, as they're not mentioned in his favourite mnemonic for remembering the traditional nine planets which definitely ends with 'pizza-pie' for Pluto; and that burning all the earth's fossil fuels ASAP was a very good thing, as left in the ground they could be extremely dangerous and burst into flames at any moment. I downed my pint and left an enlightened man.

By the time I'd got back to the guest house, the weather had closed in and the familiar wet stuff was falling. At every waking moment during the night I heard it hammering on a nearby flat roof and by morning my room's sea view had turned to rain view. Having laid out my full yellow waterproofs, I nipped down to breakfast, where all present greeted each other with 'Lovely day!' – all, that is, except the standard Eastern European waitress who greeted me with that very welcome word 'Porritch?'

Oddly, it was my trip's first porridge and came with a small jug of cream, which also seemed odd to me, but then everyone is odd about what they put on the grey globules. Adding plenty of sugar, but refraining from my usual three pats of butter, I have to say I found the cream option absolutely delicious.

Duly fuelled up, togged up and loaded up, I retrieved Tetley from Mrs Mac's shed and saddled up before the waving audience of guests peering out from their warm and dry lounge onto the guest house's rainy forecourt. I waved back and pushed off across the gravel, only to dismount again twenty metres later for the push up the busy main road out of Oban. Glancing back, I saw my early gradient defeat had caused considerable merriment back in the lounge and, though pleased to have been the source of some simple fun, my trudge out of Oban was an inauspicious start to Stage 2.

*

The northbound A85 soon flattens out and passes through a stretch of open heathland. Tetley seemed as pleased as me that we were on our way again, even though I'd foolishly burdened him with two 'improvements'. First, I'd swapped his big blue handlebar bag for a rack of panniers at the back. Being an incorrigible cheapskate, I'd borrowed these panniers only to find that they didn't fit properly on Tetley's rack, so that every loading/unloading became a painful battle with a pair of hooks that had already attacked Tetley's paintwork. And second, I'd taken advantage of a recent trip to the Netherlands to buy an expensive kickstand ('Da Kettle On' being unable to find one that fitted its own bicycle). The kickstand worked fine – on an empty bike. Loaded with its ill-fitting panniers, it toppled over. The bottom line was that Tetley + Equipment + Luggage = 27 kilograms, which, when added to my clothed self (even my hair-cut, beard-trimmed and toenail-clipped self), meant that I had to push a whopping 102 kilograms up every up-gradient and battle with overworked brakes down every down-gradient. My own fault.

Giving the brakes a good wet-weather test, I hurtled past Dunstaffnage Castle, past a wealthy-looking marina and back down to sea level at Connel, where I left the Glasgow-bound traffic to take the northbound A828.

Connel Bridge has a strange history. Built in 1901 to carry a northward branch off the Callander and Oban Railway's main line, it would also have saved an incredible 93 miles on the road journey from one side of Loch Etive to the other... except that the railway company refused to let even pedestrians use the bridge. Looking across the narrows – narrow indeed at about 150 metres hereabouts – you can't fail to see how infuriating that must have been. So the frustrated locals duly put pressure on the railway company until in 1909 it half-relented by running a single carriage on a shuttle service across the bridge and also a flat rail wagon to carry cars and carts – but at the stinging price of fifteen shillings per vehicle. What the locals really wanted was to be able to pay a reasonable toll to drive or walk across the bridge and it was only when proposals to start a chain ferry emerged in 1914 that the railway company finally gave in, but still charged extortionately high tolls and insisted, for example, that a shepherd lead his sheep across one at a time! When the branch line closed in 1966, the more common reaction of disappointment was replaced in this corner of the Highlands by wild rejoicing as Connel Bridge finally became a toll-free road bridge, as it remains today – a single-carriageway span controlled by traffic lights.

Scuttling across, I pulled up halfway to peer over the railings at the Falls of Lora – a misnomer, since they are in fact rapids: dramatic, swirling rapids caused by the waters of Loch Etive spilling over an underwater shelf as the tide ebbs away to Loch Linnhe and giving the twice-daily appearance of a major continental river. Just as I was about to remount, a glint of red down by the rapids caught my eye. Leaning over the parapet, I could barely believe what I saw: a small freighter, loaded with palletised goods, was caught in the rapids and struggling at full power, apparently to forge a way upstream – with little success, as it was gradually disappearing backwards, downstream and out of view. I quickly nipped across the carriageway just in time to see the little red vessel emerge downstream from the bridge, bumpily swing around to point its bows at last in the direction of travel and then proceed gracefully out towards Loch Linnhe. It now seemed more likely that the full-steam-ahead, sternward drift through the rapids was by design rather than accident and that maybe this was a perfectly regular manoeuvre. To a non-seafaring cyclist, though, it looked like the height of maritime folly.

Saddled up again and thanking the Callander and Oban Railway Company for saving me 92.9 of the 93 miles from Connel to North Connel, I scooted down the bridge into Benderloch. Just as the Falls of Lora are no falls, Benderloch is no loch but a small peninsula between Loch Etive and Loch Creran. Immediately over the bridge on the left lay a small airfield sporting at its entrance a big new road junction under construction. Could this be a new Ryanair destination? Connel for Glasgow?

Benderloch village arrived with an early entry for the day's funniest name – Ardmucknish House B&B – and a cafe, in which I gladly took refuge from the continuous rain. Two motorcyclists followed me in and ordered two breakfasts, only to get the response: 'We dinna do breakfasts.' It was ten o'clock in the morning in a roadside cafe: how did they earn any money? I had just a coffee and a dry-out.

On the edge of Benderloch, The Rule took me off the main road for the first time that day and onto a single-track lane past isolated white bungalows half-hidden by trees, with an air of Cape Cod about them. The road popped in and out of woodland until suddenly skirting a large dour-looking house with grey rendering that managed to look older than the house itself. This was Barcaldine Castle. It was built in the sixteenth century, one of seven castles held at that time by 'Black Duncan', Sir Duncan Campbell of Dunorchy, whose descendent Roderick Campbell ('Black Rod'?) still lives there and runs it with his family as a B&B: in fact, according to their website, the only B&B to be had in an ancient Scottish castle.

Soon after, my route rejoined the main road as it skirted the southern shore of Loch Creran, which it then followed for the next few miles, along with the disused branch railway that had been carried across Connel Bridge. There was little between the road and the loch at this point: a thin, wind-blown hedge, a narrow strip of well-watered, rich green meadow and a miserly pebble beach above the seaweed exposed by the tide. It would have been a rather forlorn landscape were it not for the ever-changing scene beyond the loch, with low-wooded peninsulas and islets sheltering little Loch Creran from the friskier waters of Loch Linnhe beyond and the endless grey hills of Kingairloch in the rain-heavy distance beyond that. The views were temporarily hidden by a dank stretch of conifers before the road emerged again into the open at Barcaldine village, where a busy stream tumbled from the higher forests to empty into the loch. By this point, I'd noticed a small crisis developing in my little red saddlebag and pulled into a bus shelter to investigate.

As another weight-saving trick, I'd torn from my map book just the three pages I needed for this stage and stored the current one in two layers of plastic atop the saddlebag. Two layers were proving insufficient protection against the Highland rain and a horrible dark stain was edging across the Grampians from the south-east corner, at the rate of about a mile a minute. Gingerly extracting the cartographic quagmire, I let it flap in the breeze for a while and then carefully wrapped it in my towel before storing it deep in the bowels of the panniers. Also suffering from the condensation was my watch, and so that went in too. Pushing off from the shelter, I was to be mapless and timeless for the rest of the day.

After only ten miles of Benderloch, I crossed the bridge over Loch Creran to leave Lorn behind and enter the territory of Appin, at the same time swapping a view of Creran's drizzly north shore for a view of the drizzly south shore I'd just cycled along. Here the trees were sparser and the shoreline broader, but the overpowering damp smell of rain-sodden vegetation was the same. This small coastal area, from here up to Loch Leven, is scattered with reminders of the inter-tribal warfare that seems to have accompanied the clan system, and so let's remind ourselves first where Scottish clans come from... or rather don't...

Not the origin of the species

When I referred earlier to eleventh-century King Duncan as the first king of 'all the Scots', the phrase was carefully chosen: he was not king of 'all Scotland'. In Celtic tradition, the *mormaer* (king) still held sway in each of the smaller kingdoms, while Duncan and each successor was merely the overlord or *ceann mòr* ('big head'). Significantly, it was not the big head who owned the land, but the *mormaer*s. Within each *mormaer*'s kingdom were *tuath*s (tribes), each headed by a *tòiseach* (chief). And which of these was the origin of the clan? None of them. Ha ha. The clans developed from a system of land ownership introduced to Scotland from, of all places, England – by the heavily anglicised 'big heads' of the Lowlands.

It was in the twelfth century that the *ceann mòr* of the time, Malcolm Canmore, listened rather over-attentively to his wife Margaret, a big fan of the ways of Norman England, and began to adopt the feudal system, whereby land ownership or overlordship was handed down from the monarch.

Well, as you can imagine, this went down a bomb in the Highlands. The *mormaer*s and *tòiseach*s were less than enthusiastic on one or two details of the feudal system – beginning with the bit where the king said 'I own everything'. Some did hang on to their territories, some were replaced by royal favourites, some conquered other territories – the

Highlands are nothing if not flexible – but the system of land ownership became essentially a feudal one, based around a clan led by the clan chief and landowner.

So far, so English. One major difference in the Highlands, though, was that a clan largely comprised one extended family, or group of families, which tended to be associated with a specific territory. This was not an area as static as implied by the 'clan map' on your twenty-first-century tea towel, but identifiable all the same: for example, the MacDonalds in much of Kintyre, the MacKays in Sutherland and the Campbells, well, all over the place actually.

The main road passes straight through the Strath (valley) of Appin, but I shot off seaward again on a seven-mile, single-track diversion around the peninsula of Port Appin. Away from the spray of passing trucks, I realised the rain had eased a little and enjoyed the luxury of cycling helmetless for a while. The fresh air rushing through less fresh hair lifted my damp spirits and I even managed a burst of 'I'm awaaaa the nooo' – to the mild amusement of two meadow-munching brown cows. By the time I squelched hungrily into Port Appin itself, though, the rain had restrengthened and I was once again fully togged up as I checked out the restaurant by the jetty where the ferry crosses the Lynn of Lorn to Lismore. Much too smart a joint for a soggy cyclist. I ploughed on.

Another couple of miles up the coast, a view opened up across seaweedy flats to a dramatic square tower isolated just a few hundred metres from the mainland on a tiny islet: Castle Stalker. Appin used to be MacDougall territory and Castle Stalker sits on the site of a former MacDougall stronghold built in the fourteenth century when they were Lords of Lorn. Not strong enough, though, as they were ousted by the Stewarts in 1388 and Stalker Castle was built in the fifteenth century by Sir John Stewart, the new Lord of Lorn (I wonder if he mowed his own). The clue to its purpose lies in the name: *stalcaire* is Gaelic for hunter or falconer and Castle Stalker was not the defensive structure I'd guessed but a hunting lodge, used by, among others, King James IV of Scotland, cousin of the Stewarts of Appin. However, the sporting Lord of Stalker had a stalker himself and in 1463, a MacDougall murdered Sir John on the steps of Dunstaffnage church, near Oban, where the latter had come to marry the mother of his illegitimate son. Dramatically, though, he survived just long enough to get through a ceremony of sorts and the legitimised son Dugald Stewart was to become the first Chief of Appin and in 1468 finally murder his father's murderer. The Stewarts were themselves later ousted by the Campbells in another bloody period that included 'the Appin murder mystery', the scenes of which we'll pass later this afternoon. The Scottish Highlands, the Middle East, Northern Ireland, Sicily... where there's tribes, there's trouble.

Rejoining the A828, I saw the village of Portnacroish was only a mile up the road. Surely it would have a cafe. Approaching past a small flock of sheep busily munching on the dripping heathland, I could see a sign: Castle Stalker View Cafe. Be open, be open. Twenty more turns of the pedal and... *Eureka!*... 'Cafe Open'! There ensued a complicated de-biking routine as I tried to get my bedraggled self into a state suitable for contact with other hominids, but eventually I was almost presentable and felt so relieved to sit down before a bowl of steaming soup and a plate of chunky fruit scone that I actually took their photograph. Remotitis. The other customers quickly paid up and left.

*

Temporarily revived, I pulled on my still-dripping gear and set off again as the road turned north-eastwards once again to hug the shore of Loch Linnhe, which emerged in all its storm-chopped glory beyond the little island of Shuna. About four miles north of Portnacroish, I pulled up by a road sign containing a magic word. After over five days' cycling in a more or less northerly direction, I was finally bidding farewell to the beautiful and bountiful county of Argyll and Bute and entering 'Highland'. If the former is enormous to parochial English eyes, then the latter must be *gi*normous, as, except for a small diversion, Highland would be feeling the weight of Tetley's tyres for the whole of the remaining route to Cape Wrath – a vast expanse of Britain encompassed in a single county and home to a mere 207,000 people, that's to say fewer than live in the small city of Derby.

What the road sign actually said was: 'Highland Council. Lochaber the Outdoor Capital of the UK™'. Not content with meaningless drivel (what's an outdoor capital?), the council undertakes the pointless task of actually trademarking it. I turned round to see what Argyll and Bute had to say to the southbound traffic: 'Argyll & Bute. Drive Safe'. One council spouts meaningless phrases, the other prefers ungrammatical ones.

Duly enlivened by my silent tirade, I pressed on along what must be one of the most boring roads in Britain: dark grey sky above, darker grey tarmac below, grey-green trees on either side – a grey universe on a grey day. Perhaps the councils' signwriters would be better employed designing one to warn traffic of: 'Boring Road Ahead.'

The rain had now become theatrical. Trucks and buses sloshed past, hurling water at me horizontally as though by a human chain of stagehands with an endless supply of buckets. Walking up the hills in my sodden shoes was like stepping through porridge. Grey porridge, of course. Near Duror, through the H_2O curtain ahead, I could just make out a car pulled over at the side of the road with its hatchback open and a middle-aged woman standing beside it. As I approached I was surprised to see her beckon to me and so pulled to a soggy halt.

'I have beeg room in car. I take you to wherever you go. You vairy wet, no?' Another Eastie.

Naturally thanking her for the kind offer, I explained my mission.

'Ah, eet's a challenge. You no cheat. Good lack. You vairy wet.'

Waving my thanks again, I pulled away. How many Brits – men or women – would stop to invite a soaking man and bike into their dry car? As a giant heron squawked overhead, the long and boring road finally emerged into open country where the black waters of Loch Linnhe worried away on my left at a little stony beach below the road. Across the water, low clouds clung tightly to the lower slopes of Kingairloch and Ardgour, but a low pass dipped below them to form a tiny saucer-shaped wedge of lighter grey. If my map-free memory was right, this was the pass I'd be heading up the next day. The hamlet from where I was surveying this scene was Kentallen, central to...

The Appin murder mystery

Even an ignorant Sassenach such as myself had begun to see a wee pattern in the historical ebb and flow of Highland politics. Whichever clan achieved a certain dominance over a certain area, it was always a temporary dominance, since one particular clan seemed persistently to stub them out in the end. That clan was the Campbells, and there was a reason for their successes: the Campbells were professional creeps. Specifically, they always managed to ingratiate themselves with the king, whether of Scotland or of Britain, from Robert the Bruce onwards. With royal approval came titles (Duke of Argyll), jobs (government representative), money and – significantly – soldiers by the sporranful.

In 1752 the government representative of the time, Colin Campbell, was shot dead near Kentallen and what followed was a classic demonstration of the unsubtle Campbellian fist. Since the central strategy of Colin C's housing policy was to throw out anyone called Stewart and replace them with anyone called Campbell, it's not surprising that a Stewart was suspected of the murder. In fact, one Alan Breck Stewart was suspected but nowhere to be found and so another Stewart – James, of Acharn, who happened to be the first Stewart encountered by the Campbell party after the murder, and who was merrily sowing oats a few fields away – was subsequently arrested instead. He was tried at Inverary by a jury packed full of Campbells and before a judge that happened to be head of the Campbell clan, the Duke of Argyll. Guess what?

James Stewart was found guilty and hanged. Whether you'd committed a crime or not, mess with a Campbell and you were in the soup. This particular sad tale of injustice was used by Robert Louis Stevenson in his novel *Kidnapped* and no, in the film the part of James Stewart was not played by James Stewart.

Only a few miles inland from here was the scene of the most infamous murders in Scotland's troublesome tribal history: the massacre of some forty MacDonalds by the ever-treacherous Campbells one cold winter's day in 1692, at Glen Coe. After the stories of the various Appin murders, it was a relief my route didn't take me there. Instead it took me across the 1975 Ballachulish Bridge.

Now, while many a football match may be a game of two halves, Ballachulish ('the hamlet of the narrows') is a place of three halves. North and South Ballachulish, now connected by the road bridge, had been linked since 1912 by a ferry, whose slipways are still visible. But two miles up the south side of Loch Leven is Ballachulish, originally called Laroch, but later picking up its current name from the nearby Ballachulish slate quarry. Confused? I was getting used to it.

The bridge propelled me over Loch Leven and therefore geographically out of Appin and into Lochaber, a vast, lofty and dramatic area that includes Ben Nevis. 'Lofty' is not an appealing word to the weary cyclist and I was pleased that the part of Lochaber I was to traverse was the merest sliver of coastline round to the village of Onich, at the point where Loch Linnhe splits into two northerly fingers.

At Ballachulish the A828 had joined the main A82 Glasgow–Fort William road and as the traffic got heavier the spray got so bad that I did something I'm forever complaining about in other people: I cycled illegally on the pavement for the last four miles to Onich. With no pedestrians visible at all, it does make you wonder why the council doesn't just put up a few blue signs, drop a few kerbs and generate four miles of very welcome and legal cycle path, shared with pedestrians as elsewhere. I know the reason can't be lack of money, as earlier in the day I'd used a very expensive but virtually pointless piece of cycle path as I'd crossed Loch Creran. At a roundabout where a very minor road joins the A828, a very short, high-quality cycle path separates cyclists from the traffic, and get this: it's double-track! All the neat white road markings are for northbound and southbound cyclists passing each other at this very spot – a circumstance that I calculated, using the sample cycle-spotting on this trip, as having a probability of 1 in 8,100.

To confirm the demand for an Onich cycle path, just before my destination a peloton of seven touring cyclists splashed by in the opposite direction, each giving me a grim grin and encouraging wave: the first cyclists I'd seen en route since the little boy at Tayinloan, over three cycling days before. While still taking in this sudden sprouting of bikes, an eighth overtook me with a brief 'Way-aye!' and shot off to the left at the turn for the Corran ferry. So did I, for this was my night's destination: the Onich Bunkhouse.

I'd been practising a Gaelic phrase or two that a friend had told me may come in handy up here: *Tha mi fuar agus fliuch. Is mise a tha furcht.* (I'm cold and wet. I'm completely buggered.) Actually, I think one of these Gaelic words may be made up. As it was, though, my debut in Gaelic had to wait as, when Way-aye and I parked our shiny wet machines inside an unfinished annex, it was with an English accent that he asked where I'd come from.

'From Oban today,' I offered proudly. 'And you?'

'Oh, Glasgow,' he said.

Glasgow was about a hundred miles away. At least the wiry Way-aye looked a bit younger than me.

To tell you the truth, I wasn't quite sure what a bunkhouse was, but had expected a dormitory of beds, each sporting a disembowelled rucksack and a pair of steaming grey socks. What I got was a light and spacious room to myself – and en suite to boot. There was another bed in the room, but with no one due to fill it I was delighted to throw my own horrible kit all over the floor and myself into the shower. Transformed into semi-human form, I delicately unwrapped my cycling towel to inspect the state of the limp rag formerly known as map: still intact, but still short of a few hours' airing. Instead of poring over the next day's route as usual, I'd have to pass the evening in the Corran Inn listening to the locals. In any case, I'd already made the key decision.

I'd had two choices for the next day's route, both of which would have initially followed a coast road. I could have trundled up the A82 to Fort William and from there shot off up the Great Glen to Invergarry to hit the coast again at Loch Duich. The reason The Rule would have allowed this is that if you head west from Fort William –

along whichever route – then, unless you take a ferry, you always end up back where you started. And the reason for *this* is what they call 'the empty quarter': the magnificently undeveloped peninsulas of Morar and Knoydart, whose only road to anywhere is the main road to the ferry port of Mallaig, the 'Road to the Isles'.

Alternatively, I could accept the inevitability of ferries and head west immediately, enabling me to enjoy the splendid peninsula of Ardnamurchan, crowned (if you can be crowned on your left elbow) by the westernmost point of the island of Great Britain. Judging from the pictures, this was exactly the sort of place I'd come all this way to see. Yes, I thought I could hear the wind calling: 'Go west, young man!' And specifically: 'Go west on the ferry across the Corran Narrows of Loch Linnhe tomorrow morning at ten past seven, young man.' All right, wind, your flattery worked.

By now I was not hopeful of encountering any locals in the bar of any Highland pub. The nearest the Corran Inn had to offer was three builders from the Lowlands, but they did prove to be pretty good entertainment. When one asked his mate for a pint of water in his round, the latter struggled:

'Two paints o' heavy and a paint o' w… w… it's nae good, I canna say it, I'm frae Dundee!'

The serious talk in the bar, though, was the weather and specifically the forecast that, with western Britain due to be battered by the tail end of Hurricane Gordon, tomorrow would certainly be even worse than today.

Chapter 6

The Last Great Geographical Discovery in Great Britain: Ardgour, Sunart and Ardnamurchan

For the third cycling morning in a row, I set off in the rain. Having to catch the 7.10 ferry meant it was too early for breakfast at the inn and so I'd breakfasted in my luxury bunkhouse room on the only things I'd been able to buy last night: peanuts and Coke.

Now here's an odd thing. All along this trip are examples of short ferry crossings having been replaced by bridges, but, despite the 47-mile route it would save, no bridge has yet ousted the delightful Corran ferry across the 500-metre Corran Narrows. Indeed, the latest vessel shuttling to and fro here, the *MV Corran*, was introduced as recently as 2001 and is financed by The Highland Council.

For this five-minute shuttle, the Corran boasts no CalMac-style buffet and bar, but does serve up some stunning views along Loch Linnhe, one of the biggest of an apparently never-ending series of north-east/south-west sea lochs in the southern Highlands. Time for a short geology lesson.

Thrusting and grinding

Any glance at a map of Scotland will tell you that its west coast is wiggly in the extreme. Despite my poor preparation for this trip, even I'd noticed this – and its consequence that you generally need to add more than the standard twenty per cent to a straight-line distance to come up with the true road distance between any place and the next one north or south. A lot more.

The main wiggle contributor is the series of sea lochs gouging great chunks out of the land, great north-east chunks by and large. This north-east/south-west 'grain' of the landscape was initially created by the angle at which two plates of the earth's crust collided about 400 million years ago, forcing up great diagonal mountain ridges that are believed to have been as high as the Himalayas are now.

After sinking below sea level and then being thrust above it once again, the 'new' Caledonian mountains, while still retaining the same 'grain', now had an overall slant down to the east from a watershed very close to the west coast. The last ice age then sent glaciers down the relatively sharp incline to the west coast, grinding out their typical U-shaped valleys along the line of the existing north-east/south-west weaknesses, before the melting ice caused the sea to rise and flood these new valleys as lochs (fjords) and sounds (sea channels), creating new islands at the same time.

This shudderingly simplistic analysis holds true only as far north as Kyle of Lochalsh. From there up to Cape Wrath things were and are very different indeed – and not just in geomorphology, it turns out.

After a toll-free ride for Tetley and me (I've no idea why), we clattered down the ramp into the fabulously Tolkienesque-sounding territory of Ardgour. In far Ardgour lies the dark peak of Throbbit, while beneath the rocks of Ardgour lurks the grey beast of Gobbit. Or something. Actually, this side of the loch is MacLean country.

The little settlement around the ferry's slipway didn't look very threatening, though, with its stumpy little lighthouse, built in 1860 by David and Thomas Stevenson, and its jolly white (and jolly expensive) 'Inn at Ardgour', from which emerged an early hiker, heavily cagouled but already wet. There's a mystery of sorts here, though. Several websites, including local tourist guides, call this village Ardgour, while all the maps I've used, including the Ordnance Survey's, call it Corran. Whatever its name, it looked a great place for sitting around and gawping at the view. With my first fifty-mile day ahead, however, I reluctantly veered left past the lighthouse and set off down the north shore, looking across three miles of blue-grey Loch Linnhe to the Appin shore

I'd ridden yesterday. As I left the village, a signpost told me its correct name was Ardgour, coming from *àrd ghobhar*, 'height of the goat'. The area of Ardgour comprises four parallel massifs stretching east–west between Lochs Linnhe, Shiel and Sunart. Most of the glens that drive between these mountains boast barely a track, the exception being the southernmost, Glen Tarbert, which – as I'm sure you expected – runs along an isthmus connecting the mainland to another peninsula: the remote land of Mordor. No, just kidding, it's Morvern.

The busy two-track road ran between affluent-looking bungalows, set in large grounds and surrounded by gentle meadows and occasional copses. I was puzzled at first why such an out-of-the-way route should have so many trucks and vans splashing past, until I remembered it led to the Mull ferry that ran from Lochaline on Morvern's far shore. (All navigation today was again from memory, my map still being in intensive care.) With the advancing day the views were finally lightening and at one beach I noticed a grey seal-shaped rock half-hidden under the shallows. An information board about half a mile further on suggested that it was more likely to have been a grey rock-shaped seal wandering a little way from its home on the Sallachan Rocks just off shore.

At Inversanda, a single-track B road continues southward along the shore to some beautiful pebble beaches where sheep wander right to the water's edge, but alas today's schedule, of which the objective was a chance of sunset from the Point of Ardnamurchan, had me turn my back on Loch Linnhe at last and head west up the A861 through

Glen Tarbert. With my heavy load I was soon out of the saddle and walking up the glen. The morning's rain, though thankfully unaccompanied by the promised storm-force winds, did bear a striking resemblance to yesterday's persistent little dripper and my shoes already felt as though they were full of cold pasta salad. Angry brown streams rushed under – and sometimes over – the road, while higher up, the smaller streams draining the dark slopes of Creach Bheinn to the south and Garbh Bheinn to the north looked like wisps of silver hair on a black head. The higher I pushed the bike, the closer around my yellow hood seemed to lurk the dark grey clouds. To keep my spirits up I found some wet-weather words for my little song:

I'm awaaaa the noooo,
I'm soak-ed through and through.
The weather could be better
But ma shirt could no' be wetter
And nor couuuuuld ma shooooe.

By the time I grunted up to the summit and stopped for a swig of water before remounting, my shoes were once again the full porridge. A surprising sight just beyond the summit was a camp of six travellers' caravans occupying what must today have been the least desirable lay-by in Britain. Ahead, the snaky form of Loch Sunart peeked its relatively bright waters in and out of the wooded slopes of Sunart and Morvern, but my eyes were for the most part fixed on the treacherous wet surface of the road as I freewheeled down to the junction at the head of the loch, re-entering MacDonald territory as I did so (according to my tea towel). Here the bursts of traffic from the Corran ferry mostly headed south across Morvern to Lochaline, eighteen miles distant, while I pedalled on westward past a sign that promised 'All Services' in the next village.

I thought perhaps I'd start with the clothes-dried-while-you-wait service, taking in the cyclists-towelled-down-and-treated-with-Deep-Heat-by-Polynesian-maidens service and then the combination-roof-and-sail-fitted-free-to-bicycles service, finishing with the Cornish-pasties-served-with-hot-Bovril-on-sunny-terrace service. Skidding hopefully into town, I spotted a cafe-with-verandah service and made straight for that. This was a substantial village boasting not just cafe but shop, garage, school, hotel and even tourist office. A pretty village, too, but one with a unique and slightly sinister history.

Throughout the western fringes of Britain, deposits of silver, lead and zinc have been mined for centuries and in the early 1700s a large operation was set up to extract these valuable minerals from the hills around the steep valley to the north of here. By 1730, 600 men were employed in the mines, some housed in this village and others up the valley in Scotstown. These included some French prisoners of war and it was they who, in 1790, came across material that was neither silver nor lead nor zinc. Investigations revealed it to be an entirely new mineral, from which in 1808 an entirely new element was isolated. This element is best known to us now through an isotope that occurs as a by-product of the fission of uranium in a nuclear reactor. This village's Gaelic name is *Sròn an t-Sìthein* ('nose of the fairy knoll') and is anglicised to Strontian. The mineral discovered here in 1790 was named Strontianite; the element strontium; and the isotope strontium 90. It seems strangely comforting that enshrined in the periodic table of the elements are the Gaelic for nose and fairy.

None of this concerned me as much as getting out of my wet togs ASAP. Having parked Tetley on the cafe's verandah, therefore, I proceeded to use him as clothes horse and wardrobe as I stripped off my top half and all of my footwear, wringing the water out of each offending item onto the gravel. So preoccupied was I with my soggy sartorial state that I didn't notice the small coach from Glasgow pull up and disgorge onto the gravel about 25 touring ladies of a certain age. Only when they began to crunch past me en route to the shop did I apologise for my crude behaviour, but most of them carefully looked the other way… except one. A short lady of about seventy, clad in turquoise hat, turquoise cape, turquoise shorts, knee-length turquoise tartan socks and, oddly, bright yellow shoes, picked a route that passed close by me on the verandah, where she said:

'Good morrrrrning tae you, young man! A fine day to tak the air, would ye no' say?'

Indeed it was, I agreed, but not too fine a day for drying clothes. This she seemed to find a very satisfactory response and descended grinning to rejoin her friends. Pleased to think I might still be a 'young man' to someone, I donned a drier – or at least less wet – set of clothes before clomping into the cafe for elevenses, which I snaffled up listening to three younger women gossiping about a forthcoming wedding, for which the bride had apparently gone to Inverness (88 miles away) for her hairdo.

Resuming my route along the north shore of Loch Sunart, I knew from reading it up beforehand that I'd soon be passing through some of the most extensive oak woods in the British Isles. At one time, coastal woodlands stretched all the way down the Atlantic shores of Europe from Scotland to Portugal and these native oaks of Sunart are being restored under a scheme partly financed by the EU. Initially, however, the main feature of the landscape was acres and acres of ferns crossed by a single line of old-fashioned, tree-trunk telegraph poles, the sort that used to march parallel to every railway line in the country. I wonder when they disappeared elsewhere and why they've survived here?

After about two miles, though, the now single-track road dived into the mixed woodland that, sure enough, did feature many an impressive oak, but also (if my shaky tree-recognition was right) birch, ash, hazel and lots and lots of rowan trees, whose red berries offered, on a day like this, just about the only splashes of colour in a dark, dank tunnel of grey-green. These woods apparently also contain a small population of red squirrels, at the extreme north-west of their range in Britain and free here from the threat posed elsewhere by the burgeoning numbers of grey squirrels. Didn't see any, though.

Out on Loch Sunart, the surface was suddenly getting choppier and a bright orange dinghy tossed repeatedly against the little jetty that secured it. It was a westerly, too, and it began to hamper my already slow progress. Time for the Fourth Law of Cycle Touring:

4: Wind and gradient are effectively the same thing.

Progress it was, though, and about a mile beyond Resipole and its idyllic-looking campsite, I entered 'the extreme west', for this point sits on exactly the same longitude as Land's End in Cornwall and therefore the entire route for the rest of the day crossed the westernmost part of the island of Great Britain: the Ardnamurchan peninsula.

It starts at Salen, where I knew from a previous trip that good food was to be had at the Salen Inn. My thoughts turned to food again.

Salen, Salen, give me your luncheon do.
I'm half starvin' all for the lack of food.
It won't be a stylish meal.
I can't afford the veal.
But coffee and sweet
My desires will meet
At a table with Salen view.

At the road junction where the B8007 heads off into Ardnamurchan, a big sign confirmed my hopes: 'Salen Inn, Cosy Bar, Good Food.' At the inn itself, a bad sign dashed them: no cars parked, no lights on, nobody around – save a blue Oban Express van that had shared my Corran ferry crossing and now made hurried deliveries at the rear.

So I trudged foodless on, before sheltering for five minutes in a red phone box where I feasted on two tic tacs and a mouthful of water. In the dry box I also risked a glance at the recovering map which told me the next lunch opportunity should be six miles ahead at the village of Glenborrodale.

About halfway there, just after I'd finally emerged from the woodlands, a strange sight had me out of the saddle and scampering across some rocks to the lochside where atop one large rock was perched a pile of slatelike stones in what could have been a cairn except that it was about fifteen centimetres across, a metre tall and leaning at a completely unfeasible angle. Closer examination showed that all the stones were held in place by a single bolt. It must have been art. Simple but effective art. I liked it. This out-of-the-way little sculpture was certainly worth a hundred of the ridiculous 'installations' that feature so often in the Turner Prize. Those pretentious metropolitan half-wits should come out to Ardnamurchan to see what art is. And then the anonymous cairn artist spoiled it for, as I cycled on, first one, then five, then scores more of these bolted stone piles decorated every other few metres of roadside wall. One or two struck me as original; after a hundred or two I felt more like striking the artist.

At the next headland, I pulled into a parking area, partly to ogle the sandwiches being scoffed by a couple sitting in their motorhome, but also to read the information board for nearby Dun Ghallain, 'the fort of the storms', built by an Iron Age chieftain about 2,000 years ago. The board also informed me that, although 'you're welcome to walk anywhere in the woodlands', they are currently 'closed for an upgrade'.

Pondering how trees could be 'upgraded' (to be compatible with the latest version of Windows?), I entered Glenborrodale – which came and went with no cafe nor even a shop, just a strangely misplaced Victorian mansion, an Outward Bound centre and a minibus from Oxfordshire, driver of which leaned out to ask after a ginger-haired lad: 'One of ours has gone missing.' (How many ginger-haired lads had they got?) Two miles beyond, though, at Glenbeg, two unexpected things happened simultaneously: a handsome lochside cafe appeared out of nowhere and it stopped raining.

With the constant drips from both my helmet and my hood, I hadn't noticed at first, but when I started taking off my togs outside the Natural History Centre (for this is what the cafe was part of), I felt a strange nothingness on my head and hands. Looking around the scene in startled disbelief, I realised that this was the first time since pulling into Kilmartin, three cycling days and 100 miles before, that nothing was falling from the sky. It was half past one and I celebrated with another revitalising lunch of soup, scone, jam and coffee before setting off again hood-, coat- and trouser-free, on what felt like the start of a completely different ride.

★

Soon after leaving Glenbeg, the B8007 veers sharply inland to avoid the 500-metre bulk of Ben Hiant. This peak, which soon casts off the soft green scrub of the surrounding country to climb grey and barren to its rocky peak, dominated both landscape and seascape before me. When perusing the route beforehand, I'd noticed the temptation of a track cutting straight across the southern flanks to Kilchoan, but one look at the vicious-looking reality of Ben Hiant told me how foolish such an idea would be. It looks this way for a reason...

Explosive times

We left the Highland's geological tale around 400 million years ago with an explanation of the north-east/south-west orientation of Loch Linnhe and most other lochs of the southern Highlands.

About 60 million years ago, Scotland was on the move again. With the rest of Europe, it was drifting away from North America as the Atlantic Ocean was being formed – as indeed it still is, with convection currents in the mantle, driven by heat from the earth's core, forming new rocks on the mid-Atlantic ridge. Recent volcanic activity of this kind has taken place on and around Iceland, but when the drift first started, the volcanoes that accompanied it included those the remains of which we still see on Arran, Mull, Rùm, Skye – and Ardnamurchan.

Ben Hiant is the remains of one of these volcanoes, but the crater of a much larger one – three miles across – can be seen further west, just inland from Sanna Bay.

As I started the climb inland, where a milepost told me that Kilchoan, the westernmost village in Great Britain, was still seven miles away, the sun finally came out and I turned to survey the scene that had opened up to the south. All the way along Loch Sunart, the opposite bank had been formed by the largely uninhabited shores of Morvern, but now an inlet opened up with, to its west, a lighthouse clearly visible and a tiny cluster of white buildings rather less so. This was the Sound of Mull and the island's capital, Tobermory. I scanned beyond the lighthouse to a heavily forested headland off which lay, so I understood, the wreck of a vessel from the Spanish Armada that basked in the grandiose name of *Santa Maria della Grazia y San Giovanni Battista*. When it showed up here in 1588, the local MacLeans offered supplies in return for some Spanish assistance in plundering the Small Isles: Rùm, Eigg, Canna and Muck. The perfidious MacLeans, however, included in their supplies one small bomb. *Adiós* Maria, *adiós* Giovanni. The bay is called Bloody Bay.

The single-track road headed on northwards and just after Loch Mudle, a final push over another brow opened up a new panorama to the north: down over the scrub and heather to a broad vale of pastureland leading to the hamlet of Kilmory and beyond that to a wide sweep of blue before the hazy but unmistakable outlines of lopsided Eigg and mountainous Rùm, two of the Small Isles that lay off Arisaig (tomorrow's destination) and heralded the beautiful views of Skye. Here's hoping the improved weather would hold.

A long freewheel down into the straggly settlement of Kilchoan (my date with the sunset leaving no time for the westernmost castle nor the westernmost ferry) and a sharp right turn for the reliable old B8007's last hurrah up to the point. About half a mile inland, I was spotted by a crouching sheepdog that sprung from his domestic lair at the chance of something to chase. Or rather lead. He bounced the way ahead, occasionally stopping to give me that get-a-move-on sheepdog stare, before being distracted by two roadside sheep, which he rapidly separated, choosing the faster as the better challenge to harry into the bracken. Just as I thought he'd wandered off, the dog burst from the undergrowth a hundred metres ahead, tongue all aflap, went to have a quick gander at a field of shaggy brown Highland cattle, thought better of it, had a quick pee, spotted me, resumed the leading chase, realised he'd meant to have a crap instead, set off again uphill, almost directly into the path of an oncoming Dutch car, spied yet another idle sheep and chased it over a few streams before disappearing forever into another patch of bracken, by now a good mile and a half from home. Who needs a wind turbine when you've got sheepdog power?

The road across the ancient volcano to the white sands of Sanna Bay had split off to the right and I was now on the route to Portuairk and the Point of Ardnamurchan. After I'd dropped off my heavy panniers at the Sonachan Hotel, where I'd be spending the night, and therefore burst out again like a sprung hare, the road split once more and, eschewing the delights of the westernmost phone box at Portuairk, I took the left option for the final two miles to the westernmost point itself.

What I didn't expect to find a hundred metres short of the Point was Great Britain's westernmost traffic light, but there it was protecting the narrow, walled and blind approach to the lighthouse and showing red. Nothing happened. Then nothing happened again. The third time nothing happened I gingerly pedalled around the curve, enjoying the smells and sounds of the ocean – quite different from a mere lochside: proper waves, proper beaches, seagulls and salt – and was welcomed into the lighthouse compound by the westernmost black dog, who encouraged me to walk across some tufts of weather-beaten grass before I discovered he was leading me to a sheer cliff. Retreat, regroup and redirect, this time up past the lighthouse to the viewing point. My hoped-for sunset over the western horizon was thwarted by the sun sinking into a low bank of cloud, but the view was still magnificent with, from left to right, the low, black hills of Coll, a broad swathe of the Sea of the Hebrides out to Barra and Uist (both too low to be visible), the mountainous mass of Rùm, the small, dark curves of Muck, the distant but unmistakable Cuillins on Skye and finally the long, jagged escarpment of Eigg. Is there a better view in all the British Isles? Nicholas Fairweather, the other coastal cyclist, declared a sense of achievement in getting here and at that moment I shared it. It felt like a definitive halfway point: between their south-west corner and their north-west corner, I stood at the western corner of the Highlands; and also the westernmost point of mainland Scotland and Great Britain. Or did I...?

I started to look at my more immediate surroundings. Now, you can call me an old stickler – and I do indulge in the occasional stickle – but according to the Ordnance Survey map (which I'd reinstated after the rain had stopped), the Point of Ardnamurchan is actually the *second* westernmost point on the British mainland. I'll pause while you take in this shattering news. About half a mile to the south, the headland of Corrachadh Mòr seemed to me to be about a hundred paces farther west. Now, I didn't get where I am today without knowing that grid north and true north are different norths and so, by the scientific method of placing my bicycle pump along the map's line for true north and then, while maintaining the pump's angle, shifting it down and along the map, I compared the claims of the Point of Ardnamurchan and Corrachadh Mòr. Mm, I reckoned Corrachadh Mòr had won it by a short tyre valve. And indeed subsequent desk-based examination has confirmed this. So I hestitate here for only this humble second before claiming this as Probably the Last Great Geographical Discovery in Great Britain: the westernmost point of our island is in fact the headland of Corrachadh Mòr on the Ardnamurchan peninsula. No tea shop there yet but it's surely just a matter of time.

The lighthouse and its visitor centre were both closed, but you could see why this light was needed. *The Statistical Accounts of Scotland of 1834–45* observes that the Point of Ardnamurchan 'from its position, is thrown much in the course of mariners'. Indeed, not only much of the local island-to-island traffic, but also any coastal route would find it difficult to avoid passing close to this point.

Ardnamurchan Lighthouse was built in 1849 by Alan Stevenson. Wait a minute – every time I mention a lighthouse I seem to mention a Stevenson. It turns out there's a reason for this...

The lighthouse family
The story starts not with a Stevenson but with one Thomas Smith.

T. Smith was suitably named, as he was a tinsmith in eighteenth-century Edinburgh who began specialising in the design and production of oil lamps for use in lighting the streets of most Scottish cities. So bright were Smith's lights that in 1887 the Northern Lighthouse Board (NLB) gave him the contract to erect four lighthouses around the Scottish coast, using oil for the light instead of the unreliable coal fires, including that on the Mull of Kintyre.

One side effect of his success with these lights was particularly significant: Smith's two wives having died, his lengthy spells away from home created something of a problem in the care of his three children. Step forward his next-door neighbour, Jane Stevenson, also widowed, who began looking after Smith's children as well as her own son, Robert. Thomas and Jane married in 1792 and two years later Robert, then 22, was appointed by his new stepfather as superintendent for the erection of the Pentland Skerries lighthouse off the Scottish north coast.

Though no blood relative, young Robert Stevenson turned out to be even more talented than Smith and, to cut a very long story very short, he became Engineer to the NLB for 35 years up to 1843, during which time he oversaw the construction of some fifteen major lighthouses, including the notoriously difficult Bell Rock lighthouse off the Scottish east coast.

Robert's eldest son Alan also starred as Engineer to the NLB, building in 1844 what many regard as the world's most beautiful lighthouse at Skerryvore off Tiree. When he stood down in 1853, two of his brothers, David and Thomas, actually shared the engineer's job and there was just no stopping the Stevensons now: they threw together another 29 lighthouses (including the one at Corran) and by this time Scottish lighthouses had become the most powerful and versatile in the world.

David's son David Alan Stevenson took over as engineer in 1885 and was still there in 1938. His brother Charles stood in for David Alan when the latter was ill and, in his spare time, almost beat Marconi to invent the wireless. Charles's son, also confusingly named David Alan Stevenson, was yet another lighthouse engineer, but took time out in a different direction, too, by publishing a book in 1959 on, yes, the world's lighthouses – in fact the book to which I referred in Chapter 1.

And finally, Thomas Stevenson's son achieved fame more widespread than all the others, although in a different field, for he was Robert Louis Stevenson.

I had to switch on my own lights as the little black dog finally escorted me from the premises. The three miles back to the hotel made it a straight fifty for the day, according to calculations from road signs rather than from my still drying map, and I'd cycled from dawn till dusk at a rattling average speed of 4.5 mph: just above normal walking pace. Even this had had me bypassing points of interest where I'd rather have loitered and so, as I rapidly showered and changed for dinner, I was already working on ways either to reduce the daily mileage or to increase this paltry average speed.

The Sonachan Hotel is Great Britain's westernmost hotel and felt like it. As I set about my westernmost fish and chips, the bar's windows rattled in the howling wind. Even here in the far west, the place was run by yet more Easties, and jolly efficient they were too. Here I was thinking that the influx of Eastern Europeans to the Highland tourist trade was a recent phenomenon, but an early 1970s guide tells me that 'You are always welcome at the White Heather Hotel, Kyleakin, Skye (Tel. Kyleakin 277), Proprietor: W. Sikorski'. The Sonachan Hotel's clientele boasted the standard three Scottish builders (this time from Oban), a fit-looking German couple, a quiet American and an English woman chatting to a local boy of about six.

'So what football team do you support, Kenny?'

'None.'

'Not Celtic or Rangers?'

'Nope.'

'Oh come on, all boys support a football team. Who is it? Hearts?'

'I dinna laik fitba.'

'But surely you have a favourite team.'

'Oooh, all rait then. Kilchoan Athletic.'

That shut the Sassenach up for a while. Kenny's main job was to keep the hotel's sheepdog Ben in order, but while his master was engaged in conversation, Ben had got bored, pulled a dog-sized Paddington Bear from the toy store and was now giving it a good seeing to, a sight that mightily impressed the builders. As the landlady turfed Ben out into the night, a gust of wind rushed in, prompting everyone to hold down their plates and glasses.

With another dawn start scheduled, I retired pretty early, falling quickly asleep, but at around midnight was awoken by voices outside my window.

'MacGinn, will ye look at the sky?'

'Wha'?'

'The stars, mon, take a look at the f★★kin' stars!'
Silence.
'Whooaargh!'
'Och, MacGinn, ye canna take yer drink, mon.'
Wishing I'd the energy to look at the stars myself, I fell back to sleep, only to be woken yet again fifteen minutes later by the roar of trees being whipped by a gale, a big crash and then a few curses as the lights went out. He was a bit later than forecast, but Hurricane Gordon had arrived. Sinking deeper into bed, I nodded off again, dreaming about a power cut stopping my pedals turning and being stranded indefinitely by a red light at the Point of Ardnamurchan.

Chapter 7

The Longest Day: Ardnamurchan, Moidart and Arisaig

It was a groggy awakening that the 6.15 alarm gave me. Another fifty-plus-mile day, much of it retracing my route along the peninsula, meant another dawn start and so I'd arranged for some bread and juice to be left in the breakfast room for me. Even better, though, the cook was already there and rustled up a coffee and a few rashers of early bacon, too. By the time I left, two of the three Oban builders were also enjoying a similar early-starter while the third – presumably MacGinn – leant grey-faced on the front door, breakfasting on a shaky cigarette.

Thankfully the wind had dropped and, on the road again, I soon made steady progress. A short way from the hotel, three black-headed gulls, each perched on an isolated post, observed my approach; two flew off before I reached them, but the third stood firm and followed my wavering passage from just a few metres away. It seemed transfixed. A mile or two along the undulating route back to Kilchoan, the builders' white van passed me with a beep and a wave, and then one more of each as it trundled in the opposite direction across the valley on the narrow road to Sanna. While the day was dry, I was not, as Hurricane Gordon's night-time attack on the electricity supply had switched off the radiator over which my cycling gear had been dangling. So this morning's sudden burst of sunshine in Kilchoan was especially welcome and eased my disappointment at the village's only shop (the post office) being closed till nine. At least that gave me a definite target for refreshment: Glenbeg's Natural History Centre.

It's an odd thing around here but these mainland massifs – Ardgour, Morvern, Ardnamurchan – seemed both more deserted and more remote than the nearby islands. For much of Ardnamurchan, the local shopping centre must still be Tobermory on the Isle of Mull, as it was in the early nineteenth century when the *Statistical Accounts* noted that 'in all of Ardnamurchan there is nothing approaching a village'.

As I left the eastern end of Kilchoan, a view across the bay opened up. Mull was clearer this morning and I could just make out a few sails in Tobermory's bay and the distant red glint of the Kilchoan ferry heading this way. It's almost the same view overlooked down on the lochside by Mingary Castle, a thirteenth-century fortification guarding the entrance to Loch Sunart, which, as with many others along this coast, changed hands between several clans before being allowed to fall into disrepair several hundred years later.

The narrow road wound up over the western flanks of Ben Hiant, giving me plenty of walking practice before cresting a rise and opening up the broad view over to the Small Isles in the north, mistier than when I'd passed them the day before. At this point, an unnumbered road shot off northwards, which was after all the way I was headed, and I can understand why Fairweather had been tempted by this route through Kilmory, Dùn Mòr and Ockle. While he ran into trouble beyond Ockle, though, I took the well-worn and conservative route around Ben Hiant and back to Loch Sunart.

The same terrain that yesterday had been decorated by gushing brown torrents as it tried to rid itself of the heavy rains was today back to its normal self: the water was clear, the streams stayed within their banks and the roads reverted to the function they were designed for and not that of supplementary stream bed. With my map reinstated atop the saddlebag I also spotted a few items I'd missed yesterday. Just after regaining the shore after the Ben Hiant diversion, the second headland eastwards bore the name I'd been waiting for all this trip. As any visitor to Scotland's west coast will know, the Gaelic for headland is *rubha*, thus speckling the map with giggly names (to an

English ear) like Rubha Aird and Rubha Mòr. And any British child of a certain age will also know the song 'Rub-a-dub-dub, three men in a tub'. I'd felt sure there was going to be one, and here it was: Rubha Dubh, 'black headland'. Unfortunately *rubha* is actually pronounced 'roo'. Shame.

Another feature I'd not noticed the previous day was that, near Glenborrodale, a footpath led into the trees to the left and up onto the high moorlands near Ben Laga before crossing to the northern side of Ardnamurchan at Acharacle or Kentra. Given the glimpses of distant views I'd been getting from the relatively low elevations of my route, what magnificent panoramas there must be up there for the walker.

One repeat pleasure, though, was the Natural History Centre's cafe, just opening at ten. Ordering my coffee and bun, I suggested that, as the only cafe along Ardnamurchan's 25 miles of main road, they might pull in a little more custom if they placed a sign at each end of the peninsula announcing that fact. They didn't seem interested. When I left, after a pleasant fifteen minutes at an outside table (what luxury!), gazing at the cows, the loch and the empty shores of Morvern, I was still their only customer.

It must have been the lack of variety in the view along the next stretch, but I'd obviously become obsessed with wayside signs again. Without the distraction of having to constantly wipe away raindrops from my specs, I noticed another mysterious one, standing on its own and proclaiming: 'This project is partly sponsored by the EU. Europe and Scotland working together.' What project? The road? The woods? The project of putting that sign up?

The wind had freshened again, veering from south-east to westerly, which put it nicely at my back, and I found myself in a race with a yacht heading up the loch near the Morvern shore. Each time I thought I'd got ahead enough to stop and photograph it, the boat had slid past again. Eventually, approaching Salen, I fell way behind and gave up the chase. In any case, it was here that I'd completed my return run along the peninsula and turned sharply north again on the A-road up to Acharacle, strung along the shores of the freshwater Loch Shiel, where I pulled in at the post office-cum-cafe for lunch.

Here I heard more about last night's storm. Apparently the power was off over a large area for several hours and some of the boats moored in Salen Bay had been tossed right over by the petulant Hurricane Gordon. It was a busy cafe with the usual Germans and Americans amongst its customers, but an unusual kitchen contingent comprising one Yorkshire woman, one Geordie and, of all things, a Scot. Not an Eastie in sight.

★

Soon after Acharacle, I entered the land of Moidart where I passed the road to Castle Tioram and then the Clanranald Bar: the two are linked. Unusually, Castle Tioram was built by a woman, Anne MacRuari, divorced wife of one of the MacDonalds, in 1353. Her son Ranald founded the Clanranald and it was a descendent of his who sided with the Jacobites in their 1715 uprising, only to have his men set fire to Castle Tioram when defeat loomed, rather than have the castle fall into the hands of the crown, in the form of their arch-enemies, the Campbells (who else?).

The run up to Loch Moidart was quite densely populated with neat little houses behind white fences and tidy hedges, most with a view over Loch Shiel and up to the solid mass of Ben Resipol. A good proportion were doing their utmost to part the passing traffic from some of its holiday funds, by advertising 'Art Studio', 'Crafts For Sale', 'Smoked Scottish Foods', 'Venison' and of course 'Rooms'. One simply guided the tourist to 'Enquiries'. For what?

The traffic had indeed increased and, now that I didn't have to turn away from the vehicles' spray, I saw that at least half comprised local white vans, carrying 'Building Materials', 'Fuel Oils', more 'Scottish Foods', 'Home Shopping' and, well, just about any commodity you might want up here. As most of the vans were shiny and new, business must be booming.

Here's a game for new visitors to the Highlands. Each time you see the name of a loch that's new to you – Loch Marmalade, say – see if you can guess five more names that appear on the map within ten miles. The peninsula on one side will probably be called Marmalade, with its headland Rubha Marmalade; the river will be the River Marmalade, the village where it flows into the loch will be Invermarmalade or possibly Lochmarmaladehead, and the main church will be at Kinlochmarmalade. There may even be a table outside the church selling 'Marmalade Marmalade £1'. But probably not.

Loch Moidart fits the bill pretty well. Just after the road swung over the River Moidart and approached a big church at Kinlochmoidart, I pulled over by a group of people leaning on a fence and staring at some beech trees on the other side of a meadow. These were the 'Seven Men of Moidart' (the trees, not the tourists), planted in the early nineteenth century to commemorate the men that Bonnie Prince Charlie brought with him from France in 1745. I suppose we'd better get the hoary old tale of the '45ers out of the way now or else it'll keep coming back like a bad curry.

Bonnie Prince Charlie and the Jacobites

Great name for a band, queer name for what they actually were.

In 1688 King James VII of Scotland (James II of England), being just too Catholic for his own good, was forced into exile in France and the joint monarchy handed first to his Protestant daughter Mary and subsequently to a series of German Protestants.

However, support for James Stewart (for his real surname was neither VII nor II) and his Catholic descendents remained strong, particularly among the Highland clans, and these supporters were referred to – bizarrely, it seems to me – as 'Jacobites'. The argument goes that Roman Catholicism was the Latin religion, the Latin for James is Jacobus and giving them a Latinised name was a kind of insult. A bit like calling German 'Krauts', I suppose. Sounds pretty weird to me – what's the Latin for Jacob?

Anyway, Jacobites they were and Jacobites they stayed, ever hopeful of a return to Scotland by their favourite. However,

James died in 1701 and his son James Edward Stewart arrived in Scotland too late to give a boost to the 1715 Jacobite uprising, which was defeated by government troops under the command of the Duke of Argyll – yes, any chance of a fight and the Campbells would be in there.

Next up was James Edward's son, Charles Edward Stewart, who landed on the shores of Loch nan Uamh on 25 July 1745. Whether or not he was actually bonnie, Bonnie Prince Charlie wasn't the first Jacobite leader to pick up that nickname, although it's possible the earlier Bonnie Dundee was so called because his men had shown little enthusiasm to follow into battle a man called Graham of Claverhouse.

You wouldn't have bet on Bonnie Prince Charlie getting far in the old rebellion business: he arrived, we are told, with only seven companions, spoke no Gaelic (having been born in Rome) and had little military experience. In the thirty years since his father's failed return, access to the Highlands had been improved by the government's military roads, and loyalty to the monarch, by now German George I, had grown in the Lowlands. Moreover, the promised support from English Jacobites had failed to show up and so he initially led fewer than 15,000 clansmen to the south, with London as their ultimate goal.

Things went surprisingly well, though, and following a military victory at Prestonpans, near Edinburgh, Charlie and his men marched into England where they got as far south as the Trent at Swarkestone, Derbyshire – indeed, recent findings suggest they may have crossed the Trent and penetrated as far as sunny Loughborough – before the overwhelming threat of government forces finally persuaded Charlie to retreat northwards, hotly pursued by an army under the Duke of Cumberland.

Cumberland trounced Charlie's lot at Culloden, near Inverness, in April 1746 and Charlie fled, with a £30,000 price on his head and a trail of death and suppression in his wake, eventually leaving Scottish shores forever on 20 September 1746 – from the shores of the very same Loch nan Uamh, in fact.

Charles Edward Stewart, 'the young pretender', died in 1788 in Rome, where he'd been born 68 years earlier. The Jacobite cause gradually died too... although you can still get a fine pie and tea at 'The Jac-O-Bite' on the shores of Loch Duich.

At the time of my trip only four of the seven beech trees were still standing – and one of those was dead. Ever faithful to the cause, however, some locals have planted new saplings to replace the old.

A hilly and heavily forested section followed, with glimpsed views across Loch Moidart to the small island of Shona that blocks its outlet to the open sea. The road reared up and over the main peninsula of Moidart before spitting me out at the glittering, broad bay of Glenuig, a definite 'Wee-ha!' moment for any cyclist who skids to a halt after many miles of lochs and glens to take in the open views across the Sound of Arisaig to the Small Isles, now much nearer than when I'd last seen them from Ardnamurchan. Bright white pebbles led down to the rippling, metallic-blue waters of Glenuig Bay itself, which edged around a gently sloping, tree-lined headland to the left before opening out into the deeper blue of the Sound that reflected the grey bases of a benign bank of fair-weather cumulus. Some twelve miles away, sandwiched between the sea and the cloudline, the horizon was filled with the low, dark blue mass of the Isle of Eigg and apparently sitting on top of this, but actually half as far away again, were the jagged grey teeth of the wild peaks of Rùm. I sat on the pebbles for a while to take it all in, while a fisherman repaired some ropes on a bobbling blue boat a few hundred metres away. Once again, the route hadn't disappointed and had come up with another spot I'd hoped and planned for.

After five or ten minutes I set off again, suitably recharged. Loch Ailort, the next one on my hymn sheet and which would dominate the views for the next eight miles or so, could easily have looked quite different from the tranquil inlet it is today. When the West Highland Railway was surveying its route from Fort William to a new railhead for access to the Isles, its first choice for the new port was a site on the south shore of this very loch, near Roshven Farm. However, the railway company and the landowner couldn't agree terms and so the railway went instead up to Mallaig, where the new dock opened up for business in 1901 and which therefore became the terminus for the modern-day Road to the Isles, the A830.

I could see both road and rail in the distance. The West Highland Railway diverges from the Oban line at Crianlarich in Stirlingshire and shoots north across the desolation of Rannoch Moor before sneaking around the massif of Ben Nevis and descending into Fort William, from where it runs more or less parallel to the A830 and eventually pulls to a weary halt at the buffers in Mallaig. It was one of the last Victorian railways to be completed. Only seven years later, it was absorbed by the North British Railway Company, an arch-rival of the Caledonian Railway that ran the Oban line. Today, services still run to and from Glasgow, as well as many an enthusiasts' excursion, notably those hauled by the 'Jacobite' steam locomotive.

Struggling up to the junction with the main road, my limbs were beginning to complain again and it was a weary and ragged cyclist that begged a pint of lemonade at the bar of the Lochailort Hotel. This seemed to be the only building in the settlement of the same name, but I'd have happily checked in if I hadn't got a rigid schedule that needed me to be in Arisaig that night, in order ultimately to be on a train at Strathcarron on Sunday, a train for which a ticket lay in my wallet. Noting that my destination lay nine miles down the road, I urged the old legs over the old saddle again – well, just one of them actually – and creaked onto the main road.

It was like the busy roads around Oban again with all sorts of traffic thundering by my right ear: a Spanish bus, a German bus, a classic orange VW camper, vans and trailers of all shapes and sizes. After a rare minute-long gap, I heard an unusually deep and throaty engine approaching slowly behind me before an old black MG passed. Then another, then another (well, perhaps they weren't all MGs actually) and then what was definitely a bright red Morgan. All had their tops down and at the wheels of these vehicles sat pairs of anciently clad sporting types: flat caps and cravats, flapping scarves and pointy sunglasses, one black bowler and not a seat belt in sight. Exceptionally, the red Morgan seemed to carry only its driver, whose woolly cap didn't quite hide his neat grey hair and who grasped the wheel with an air of confident authority: surely the team leader and – I felt certain – known as Captain Morgan. Where could they all be going?

They'd all passed me on the smooth surface of a new, wide carriageway, but soon the Road to the Isles shrank to single-track as it dived into a series of narrow twists and turns that ducked in and out of the woodlands of South Morar, playing hide and seek with the coast and the route of the railway. Halfway along, road and rail temporarily dip down to the north shore of Loch nan Uamh near 'The Prince's Cairn', supposedly marking the spot where BPC came and went.

With the hilly terrain I found myself once again getting off to push every few minutes and with one sudden descent from the saddle, I startled a hare who loped deeper into the bushes for protection. To distract myself from my pinging back and neck, I did a few more en-route sums with the conclusion that on an average Highland day I got on and off the bike about 200 times. At this end of the day, with each 'off' I told myself 'Admit it, man, you're too old for this kind of caper – get a motorhome'; but then with each 'on' it was 'Isn't this better than carpet slippers and *Match of the Day*?'

I finally passed a 'Welcome to Arisaig' sign, followed immediately by the more surprising 'Beware of Bicycles'. A cycle path appeared from nowhere, sending me scuttling over to the wrong side of the road and then back again before ditching me in the middle of what looked like a secure retirement compound in Florida. This must be Arisaig.

★

Mrs Mac's B&B was a private house, hidden in a beautiful spot a mile down the road to Rhu along the south shores of Arisaig's natural harbour, Loch nan Ceall. The sun being not long from its bedtime and the rumour being that the local pub stopped serving food quite early, I rapidly ditched my day togs, scrubbed myself down, donned my 'evening wear' (the same crumpled shirt and floppy trousers every night) and remounted for the short spin back to town, using clothes pegs as cycle clips.

Facing the harbour, by now a golden reflection of a golden sky, 'town' turned out to be a single row of buildings, comprising shop, restaurant and pub. All you need, I would have thought. Wondering what entertainment the locals would serve up for me tonight, I locked up Tetley and burst into the bar, where two silent couples and one silent male reader briefly looked up to see what had disturbed their peace before looking back down at carpet or book, still in silence.

'Evenin'.'

'Urr.'

All through my spaghetti and pint, the only sounds were pages turning, pasta whirling and beer being slurped. The couples, who weren't very old, must have already said to each other all they had to say in life and lost the will to say anything at all to anyone else. I was about to set off back to the digs when a series of 'herrumphs' and 'ahas' heralded the bustling arrival of four boisterous, forty-something Scotsmen, who addressed the barman as 'My mon' and proceeded to rearrange the bar's furniture to meet their requirements. I ordered another pint of heavy and sat back, pretending to read but in fact all ears to the newcomers' banter.

It quickly became clear that all four were doctors. They were not only well-spoken but also well-connected and their loud discussions, which were generally based around sharp but friendly disagreements, started off with the logistics of accommodating patients (or 'beds' as they called them) and the business sense (or lack of) in the current NHS regime, before moving on to the chances of 'Tommy' making it 'right to the top' and the popular subject of who amongst the four of them would have the most immediate impact as Scotland's First Minister.

There was a lot of debate about the best bet for a decent bottle or two of wine 'in these parts', before the topic changed dramatically to the engineering differences between the Suez and Panama Canals and the best way of chartering a boat to Tierra del Fuego. Only then did I notice their footwear: four pairs of wellington boots of varying size and colour. It seemed most probable that these old doctoring friends were on a boating holiday and just possible that a dram or two had already been consumed on board before sunset.

Having learnt that the NHS is the third biggest employer on the planet – after the Red Army and the Indian Railways – I gathered up my bits and pieces and left. Even though they'd taken some of the seats from my table, I don't think the merry doctors had noticed any of the other customers at all.

Back at Mrs Mac's, I saw on the box that the tail end of Hurricane Gordon had also played havoc with the Ryder

Cup in Ireland, before I sank down into the big, soft bed, alarm primed for 5.15 a.m. and the shipping forecast, for the next day was to include a sea crossing.

Tetley the bicycle sun-bathing at Port Corbert, with a view back towards the Mull of Kintyre.

The early-morning sun glints off a line of medieval grave slabs in Kilmartin churchyard.

Arresting sculpture by the banks of Loch Sunart near Glenborrodale.

Rùm, Muck and Eigg lurk behind Ardnamurchan Lighthouse's old foghorn.

And the only one along the main road through Ardnamurchan, too: the Natural History Centre's cafe at Glenbeg.

Self-service at Salen.

The sun sets over the Isle of Eigg, as seen from Arisaig harbour.

Someone left Balmacara beach, on Loch Alsh, without taking their shells.

Pass if you dare: Highland cattle near Plockton.

You have been warned.

Dwarfed by the mighty landscape of Bealach na Bà (the Pass of the Cattle), the Sage trudges on.

An abandoned house on the suitably named Destitution Road, near Ullapool.

Parking for cycles only at Enard Bay. Note telegraph pole below high tide line.

The award-winning Drumbeg Stores shows how to pull in the customers.

Part of the John Lennon Memorial Garden, Durness. The slabs contain Durness-related lyrics.

Cows on holiday on the beach at Durness.

Chapter 8

The House of the Golden Curtain: Morar, Sleat and Lochalsh

I awoke stiff-limbed and aching, having forgotten in my exhaustion to apply the old Deep Heat. Belatedly I did so now and am pretty sure Mr Mac smelled my approach to the breakfast room before I appeared. He'd said that, as he habitually rose early anyway, he'd be pleased to get my breakfast at the same time as his. On a clear dawn like today's, the conservatory where breakfast was taken, overlooking the boats moored in the bay, was certainly a splendid place to start the day and I made a mental note to return here one day with more time to loiter.

No such luxury today. One option was a 54-mile adventure including a spectacular mountain pass and I wanted to keep it open. So I pushed off again just after dawn, seeing Arisaig in the daylight for the first time. The Rhu road ran alongside the loch and the only sounds were the ripple of nearby wavelets, the cry of distant birds and the steady thud-thud of an early-morning jogger.

In the nineteenth century, Arisaig had been the terminus of the modern-day Road to the Isles, with passengers and freight transferring here to ferry services. With the railway terminating at Mallaig in 1901, a new road extension followed it and Arisaig lost most of its ferries, becoming first just a village en route and now not even that, as another new road bypasses the beautiful waterfront completely.

John Lister is unusually critical about Arisaig, which he calls 'an undistinguished little village'. His ire seems to be focused on the 'sea of tents, caravans and attendant clutter', observing that before these 'monstrosities' arrive each year, 'the seals and the herons will still be there and the cry of the curlew may still be heard; then, and only then, is the time to go to Arisaig'. That was the 1970s. Today no tent nor caravan was to be seen – either September was too late or they'd all gone to Benidorm instead.

The old road from Arisaig to Mallaig is still there and is certainly the better route if you have time, as it wiggles in and out of some gorgeous little coves and gives the traveller access to the dramatic White Sands of Morar, which are indeed just that. This traveller, however, was still not really awake and, with my mind set on a date with a ferry in Mallaig, I shot off up the new A830 bypass, which at this time in the morning was blissfully vehicle-free for the first twenty minutes. It was nearer Morar than Arisaig that I realised I'd sleepily broken The Rule: I should have been on the coast road. I pulled onto the gravel at the side of the road and considered my position. There was no way to get down there from the bypass and turning back to start again from Arisaig would mean a later ferry and an impossibly late arrival at that night's destination of Avernish, where I was definitely expected. Damn! The fact that I'd already driven along the coast road a few years before didn't help. The fact that neither the wheeling seagulls nor the early motorcyclist that swooshed past, nor indeed anyone else on the planet knew that I'd broken The Rule unnecessarily for the first time, didn't help. Head hung low, I remounted. Head raised slightly, I caught the warmth of a sunbeam on my right temple and pushed off northwards again. Head loping rhythmically from side to side, I decided to put my small aberration in a small mental box labelled 'Never Mind' and let the joys of the route ahead bury it.

The first joy was not far ahead and was Britain's shortest river, the half-mile River Morar, which is as wide and full as any Highland river and drains Britain's deepest freshwater lake: Loch (you guessed it) Morar. At 328 metres, it is deeper than Loch Ness. If a CalMac ferry the size of the one currently sailing from Mallaig to Skye were to sink and turn on its side, you could get 23 of them on top of one another and still not break the surface of Loch Morar.

The village of Morar has a neat, white little railway station and a rather expensive hotel, the car park of which, as I passed, was occupied by Captain Morgan and his cravat-toting sports car enthusiasts, the very same who had overtaken me the previous evening. This morning they were busy polishing away at the loves of their lives, removing every squashed Highland fly before setting off again to gather some more. The Captain's own machine was parked nearest the road and looked quite at home in the Highlands.

The Morgan Motor Company makes all its vehicles to order and I once visited their factory in Malvern Link, Worcestershire, with a friend in her own dark brown Morgan. At the sound of our arrival, the men in the nearest workshop came out to greet us:

'Hello, Jane. Hello, sir.'

'I thought you hadn't been here before, Jane.'

'I haven't. They just know all their machines and who owns them.'

Impressive.

I entered Mallaig through the jumble of commercial premises that seems to be bolted on to every west coast port. At the back of the police station a neatly turned out policewoman was polishing the flies off her car's blue light. Mallaig is a proper harbour town with a substantial fishing fleet as well as a marina and the Caledonian MacBrayne ferry terminal.

Now, this trip was supposed to be along the mainland coast and I'd known from the very start that my greatest obstacle would be the stretch of coast just north of here: the remote, inaccessible and almost empty land of Knoydart, cut off from the rest of the world by the Sound of Sleat to the west, Loch Nevis ('loch of heaven') to the south, Loch Hourn ('loch of hell') to the north and, to the east, a series of mountains crossed only by uncyclable tracks. In the whole of Knoydart's 55 square miles, there are only some seventy residents. More relevant to my task, there's only one surfaced road and − get this − it's a dead end at *both* ends. Yes, apart from a few steep and unsurfaced tracks, the only way in or out of Knoydart is by boat, and the only scheduled one is a small private ferry from Mallaig to Inverie on Loch Nevis. So even if I set foot and wheel in the south of Knoydart, the only predictable way out would be back the same way again.

However, things may already have changed by the time you're reading this. I'd been hoping to arrive in Knoydart via the eastern mountains along one of the new cycle tracks that contribute to Sustrans' nationwide network. According to my map, Cycle Route 78 from Invergarry to Glenelg and Skye was 'proposed' and so I'd contacted Sustrans to get the latest news. They were extremely well informed and informative but, alas, information was all they could offer, as Route 78's missing link, from Kinloch Hourn to the Glenelg road, had recently (2006) been 'placed on the back burner'. Keep an eye out, though − it'll be a spectacular one.

In a similar position, Fairweather had taken his chances and managed to cadge a lift in a tiny open boat across Loch Hourn to Arnisdale. But, with the day now looking set fair and with the gentle beauty of the Inner Hebrides' biggest island lying tantalisingly across the western horizon, I was happy to be going across the sea to Skye.

Leaning Tetley against the wall of the CalMac booking office, I went in. I was the only customer.

'Morning. One and a bike to Armadale, please. Quiet today?'

'Yes, sir. Suits me…'

(Throb)

'… fine.'

(Throb throb beeeep!)

'Wha's tha'? Oh God, I hope they've got a group booking.'

Turning, I saw Captain Morgan and the Cravats chugging into the waiting area. Taking my tickets, I made myself scarce by strolling over to the fishing harbour for a vacuum-flask coffee and cake. By the time the *MV Coruisk* was approaching and I was back at the quayside, 25 or so classic cars were all lined up to board, their occupants scattered around like basking seals, taking the sea air. The Captain was at the head with his shiny and fly-free red Morgan, but the group's organiser seemed to be a chap with a clipboard, a white tee shirt advertising 'Sun + Surf Bungalows Resort' and, of all things, a back-to-front baseball cap. Surely not quite the style, old boy? Clipboard Man drove a smart red and cream Austin Healey 3000 Mark III. Indeed, my car-spotting skills had been poor, for the most common were not MGs at all but Austin Healeys of various vintages. The last to pull in line, though, with a dramatically smashed windscreen, was a Ford Cortina Mark I. All front bumpers carried a big, sporty-looking badge, the sort you expect to say 'Monte Carlo Rally 1963' but which here declared 'Highland 3-Day Classic Tour 2006'. I subsequently discovered they were from the Lancashire Automobile Club.

The *Coruisk* was now alongside and, having been waved on first, I quickly tied Tetley up with the ropes provided and scuttled upstairs to watch the rally board: first Captain Morgan, then Clipboard Man and then hoi polloi. As we left Mallaig, the Cravats all gathered on the foredeck, the ladies in their pointed shoes and sheepskins, to admire the morning views of Skye ahead and their motors down below, while the few other passengers and I sat aft, to marvel at the sun rising behind the blue-grey hills of Knoydart. 'The empty quarter' looked at once deserted and beguiling, its peaks mostly bare, with dark forests nearer the shore and some very tiny, very isolated white houses on the shoreline itself.

What we were crossing was the Sound of Sleat (pronounced 'slate') and, as I peered up the sound, I could just catch sight of the Sandaig lighthouse which sat on the tree-lined north shore of Loch Hourn, just beyond an invisible boundary. While the CalMac ferry route falls in Malin, the lighthouse is just inside Hebrides. I'm talking shipping areas. It was the first such change on my trip: Area Malin, named after Malin Head in Ireland, encompasses the southern half of the Scottish west coast; Area Hebrides the northern half. The boundary line is a line of latitude passing through Tarskavaig, on the west side of Skye's Sleat peninsula, and out to a point in the North Atlantic way beyond the Outer Hebrides, where it gives way to Area Rockall.

Occasional rain. Good.

While the Stevenson family was doing its bit to save mariners' lives near the shore by putting up lighthouses, one man devoted the latter part of his life to laying the foundations for a service that would eventually do the same out at sea. That man was Vice Admiral Robert FitzRoy.

By the time he was appointed the first director of the Meteorological Office in 1853, FitzRoy had already had a busy life: commanding the *Beagle* on the South American voyage that transported Charles Darwin to his discoveries, being challenged to a duel by the man he had just beaten to become MP for Durham, defending the rights of Maoris while Governor of New Zealand...

It was a time of rapidly improving communications. The weather stations that FitzRoy set up around Britain's coast sent their readings to the Meteorological Office using the newly invented Morse code. From this data FitzRoy devised a daily synoptic chart, from which he derived a prediction for the approaching weather that was printed in the nation's daily newspapers, a service for which he adopted the term 'weather forecast'. The Great British public naturally began to assess its usefulness and indeed FitzRoy himself knew that the forecasts could and should be more accurate. Despite putting himself under great pressure to this end, he was ultimately frustrated by his own efforts and this, it is thought, together with the deaths of his wife and daughter, drove FitzRoy to suicide in 1865.

The seed, however, had been sown and the Met Office made steady improvements to its forecasts. Noting that deliveries at sea had proved to be beyond the range of even the most zealous newspaper boy, they began broadcasting weather forecasts on BBC Radio in 1922 and forecasts for shipping in 1924. For this purpose, the waters around the British Isles were divided into thirteen shipping areas. The shipping forecast is now updated and broadcast four times a day on Radio 4: at 00.48, 05.20, 12.00 and 17.55 – and uses a system of 31 shipping areas, extending from Iceland and Norway in the north to Portugal in the south.

In February 2002, Area Finisterre was renamed Area FitzRoy in recognition of the man on whose work this life-saving service is based.

It was a long time before I discovered why the reader of the shipping forecast thought that 'occasional rain' was 'good'. It turns out that the comment 'good', 'fair', etc. refers to the visibility and that 'good' means more than five nautical miles. That morning's forecast for Area Malin was 'South-east, backing east, 4 or 5, occasionally 6. Showers. Good.'

Here in the sheltered Sound of Sleat there was barely a swell and the clouds lurking beyond Knoydart's Ladhar Bheinn still looked fair-weather ones to me. In fact this day I got no showers at all. Good.

Disembarkation at Armadale was a noisy, klaxonic affair, with much hurrahing as one of the Austin Healeys needed the assistance of a Scimitar's jump lead to disembark at all. I'd had a word with the Scottish driver of the smashed-windscreen Cortina (stone from lorry yesterday) and learned that they'd got another 400 miles to go and that tonight's target was Applecross – so they'd be taking on a climb that lay on my own route and whose gradients were already causing me some trepidation. Not a place to stall.

It was quite a relief to be in the saddle again on the quiet roads of Skye. The island that many consider the jewel of the Hebrides is effectively a collection of peninsulas tied together in the middle by the Cuillin Hills, which rise to nearly 1,000 metres and adorn many a picture postcard and coffee-table book of British mountains. Armadale sits near the end of the southernmost peninsula of Sleat. Approaching across the Sound, I'd noticed that the hills of Sleat, though relatively low, still hid the Cuillins, unless their peaks were lost in the western haze.

Hugging the eastern shore of Sleat, the A851 had already carried almost all of the ferry traffic north to Skulamus, where it would either turn right to the Skye Bridge and back to the mainland or left to the rest of the island and maybe up to Uig on Skye's Trotternish peninsula, from where another CalMac ferry route serves the Outer Hebrides. So for a while I had the quiet but incredibly well-maintained road to myself. Virtually the entire fifteen-mile route had recently been widened, redrained, resurfaced and, for one stretch, even resited. It was no surprise to see an EU sign or two. The Highlands and Islands must vie with Ireland to be the most subsidised corner of Europe. If you're reading this in a traffic jam on a potholed commuter route somewhere in urban Europe, then be reassured that your taxes have not been lost, but are supporting the odd few vehicles that trundle across the Inner Hebrides each day.

Small, intimate wooded areas fringed the road as tiny hamlets came and went. One large and impressive complex of buildings bore a name in Gaelic only – Sabhal Mòr Ostaig ('Ostaig's big barn') – and was, I subsequently discovered, a centre for learning through the medium of Gaelic only.

As good a point as any, then, to take a closer look at the language of the Gaels.

Celtic ranges far

If you think your family tree is complicated, try the family of Celtic languages. English is one of the giant Indo-European family and so was Proto-Celtic, spoken about 2,000 years ago from the Bay of Biscay to the Black Sea by – guess who? – the Celts, Celtic people being defined as those who speak a Celtic language. Proto-Celtic divided into four families: Celtiberian, spoken in Iberia; Gaulish, spoken in Gaul and points east; Brythonic, spoken in Brittany, Cornwall, Wales and Pictland; and Goidelic. Goidelic split into Old Irish and Manx and, as we know from way back in Kintyre, Old Irish arrived in these parts on the back of, or rather in the mouth of, Colum Cille and his chums; and here it developed into Scottish Gaelic.

Got it? Scottish Gaelic, son of Old Irish, son of Goidelic, son of Proto-Celtic, son of Indo-European. After years of decline Scottish Gaelic is enjoying a renaissance and nowadays around 86,000 people speak it, the vast majority being bilingual with English. It is not, however, one of the 23 official languages of the EU (unlike Irish), nor does it have any legal status in the UK (unlike Welsh).

By the way, the Gaelic for Gaelic is *Gàidhlig*, the Gaelic for English (the language) is *Beurla* and the Gaelic for Englishman is, of course, *Sasunnach*.

At Camas nam Mult ('bay of the castrated ram') I sat on a shiny new crash barrier to have a coffee, an 'oatie and raisin cinnamon cookie' and a gander at the view. A bright green field of sheep (castrated or not) ran down to a small bay of seaweed with a ruined tower perched darkly at its head. This was the remains of Knock Castle, a fifteenth-century stronghold in the hands, at various times, of the MacLeods and the MacDonalds. Beyond the tower, the Sound of Sleat sparkled in the mid-morning sun as it stretched up to the Kylerhea narrows, hidden beneath a ring of purple hills: Ben na Caillich on Skye, the hills of Lochalsh, two of the Kintail's Five Sisters and Ben a' Chapuill on the peninsula north of Loch Hourn.

Actually, 'Kylerhea narrows' is tautological as 'kyle' comes from the Gaelic *caol*, meaning narrow. Until the railway from Inverness to Kyle of Lochalsh was opened in 1897, the crossing at Kylerhea formed the main route from the mainland to the Isle of Skye, across the narrowest point of the sound, where a south-flowing glacier had separated Skye from the mainland about 20,000 years ago. In fact this was the western end of the *original* 'Road to the Isles'.

Led by the nose

The Road to the Isles was originally a cattle drovers' route. Up to 8,000 cattle a year would be brought from the Outer Hebrides as well as from all over Skye to Kylerhea, where at low tide they would be made to swim across. The cattle would be tied together, nose to tail, usually in groups of five, and be hauled across by a rope from the front beast's nose to a leading boat, in which sat the drover. Up to twenty groups of cattle a day were led across the narrows in this way.

Their destination was the cattle markets of the south, notably Crieff and Falkirk, and two main alternative routes were taken across the hills, the split coming at Galltair. The southern route followed the coast to Arnisdale and then via Loch Hourn and Loch Quoich to Invergarry. The northern option headed over the Màm Ratagan to Shiel Bridge and on to Loch Cluanie.

So, though the drovers doubtless returned by the same route – and, we hope for their sake, without cattle in tow – it turns out that the original Road to the Isles was really forged as the Road from the Isles.

Now, here's another odd thing. The big chunk of mainland over which the drovers' route passed, between the Sound of Sleat and Shiel Bridge, is very clearly another peninsula (just look at any map), but this one seems to be nameless. Its companions to the south are Moidart, Morar and Knoydart, but this poor thing doesn't seem to have a name at all. Or if it has, I don't know it. So, until I consulted the Sage of Avernish that evening, it would have to be 'Dunnodart'.

The enchanting scene across the sound to Dunnodart had set me day-dozing for a few minutes – or maybe the cinnamon cookie was drugged with some secret Highland potion. It was certainly delicious and, coming round from my reverie, I glanced at the packet to see which remote crofter had baked it for me: ah, 'Made in Huddersfield'.

The long, smooth run up to Skye's north coast was uneventful, except for the sort of event that a cyclist doesn't really want: the sight of two motorbikes' headlights charging at you from the opposite direction at clearly illegal speeds. It became obvious before they roared past at about a hundred that the morons were actually racing each other. As they drew level, I pointed at my brain to indicate which of their organs was missing and then waited for the screech and crash that would distribute the rest over the countryside. None came, just a screech of protest from a swooping hawk.

A view to the left took in the misty, brooding Cuillin Hills and the nearby waters of Loch Eishort, which reminded me I'd reached the neck of Sleat and was entering the bulk of Skye. A short freewheel into the outskirts of Broadford brought me to the very busy A87, where I turned right. More 'classic' vehicles chugged along here, but less sleek than those of Captain Morgan and the Cravats: AEC, Foden, Potts & Sons, Pollock Ltd... classic lorries had evidently also chosen the Highlands for their 2006 rally.

Sitting on a gate with a map at Skulamus, looking over the Inner Sound to Raasay and Applecross, I had a decision to make. Tonight's destination was a tiny hamlet near Dornie, where, at the House of the Golden Curtain, lives the Sage of Avernish. I'm not the only one of the Sage's friends who uses this nickname, so appropriate is it to a man who, though still in early middle age, exudes such an air of carefully acquired knowledge that I'm always more than fifty per cent confident that he'll be able to answer whatever question I ask. As a local, his hit rate should be even higher for the questions I'd been storing up this time.

The preferred route was up and over Glen Arroch, across the water on the little Kylerhea ferry, past Glenelg, through Dunnodart, up and over Màm Ratagan, through Shiel Bridge and along the shores of Loch Duich: six hours.

The other option was along the main road, over the Skye Bridge, through Kyle and along the shores of Loch Alsh: three hours. While I'd temporarily left the mainland, The Rule made no sense and so both options were allowable. It was two o'clock. Màm Ratagan would mean arriving at the Sage's door, and probably somewhere near death's, in the dark. I was not yet tired but very hungry. There was a caff up the road.

Yes, it turned out to be an easy decision.

After pedalling a few hundred metres to the Crofter's Kitchen, I settled down to a relaxing omelette, chips and *The Guardian*. The only unique experience I was sacrificing by this decision was the chance to see what is meant by 'the last hand-operated turntable ferry in the world' (a website's description of the Kylerhea ferry). Actually, my omelette and chips weren't all that relaxing as the cafe's waitress, although another Eastie, was not the discreet and super-efficient variety I'd become accustomed to, but so effusive and disorganised that none of the customers could concentrate on their food. Though in her forties, she wore Swiss-style plaits behind a doll-like face and wore a check apron over an Alpine-length skirt. Heidi greeted everyone as though she'd known them since childhood, taking such pains with each new order that she completely forgot all the previous ones. The frequent grunts and calls that came from the kitchen served only to distract Heidi further. I distracted myself as well as I could in the first newspaper I'd read for days.

★

From Skye-side, the Skye Bridge appears all of a sudden. A sign said 'Cyclists Dismount' but, with no further advice as to what to do next, I waited what I trusted was long enough out of the saddle, smiled at the camera, flapped my arms and cycled over the bridge. It was opened in 1995, replacing the heavily used Kyleakin ferry, and after a long and bitter battle by the locals finally went toll-free in 2004. The view on all sides is spectacular, taking in, to the north, Scalpay, Raasay and Applecross as well as Skye; to the south, a fabulous panorama along Loch Alsh as far as the glen that contains Loch Duich, closed out by a horizon that bristles with the mountains of Skye, Kintail and, er, Dunnodart. The motorist can barely glance at a sliver of this and walkers need to tramp a couple of miles to get there and back, but the cyclist can take it all in at leisure.

As I swung the leg over again, who should throb across eastbound but Captain Morgan? Sans Cravats. The Cravats must have called in somewhere on Skye for lunch and the Captain was either very early or very late getting away for the struggle up to Applecross. I remember a television programme in the dim, black-and-white past where a series of muddy Morgans competed to get furthest up an absurdly steep and horribly muddy incline, encouraged by a screaming Murray Walker. The Applecross ascent must have been something like that.

Kyle was sunnily busy with Saturday afternoon shoppers. Like Mallaig and the southern end of Oban, this port has also managed to assemble an ugly jumble of buildings to share its heart-stoppingly beautiful view: in this case, the dramatic rise of Skye across the narrows. Kyle's one architectural compensation is the bridge itself, its graceful span enhancing the view both from the town and all along the north shore of Loch Alsh.

After loitering in Kyle till the midges, who weren't supposed to be here this late in September, started midging around my head, it was along the A87 Loch Alsh road that I continued. Having briefly pulled over at five o'clock in front of a football pitch with two oddly tall goalmouths to hear the day's results from elsewhere on my little radio ('Di-da-di-diddly-da-di-da-di daa-daa-daa...'), it was about a quarter past when I drifted into a familiar front garden in Avernish, to be greeted by the Sage and Rosemary. The House of the Golden Curtain saw my first daylight finish since Oban.

★

The Sage and his wife both work and, with another guest this weekend in the Sage's daughter, must have been up to their eyes. Nevertheless, immediately after I'd checked that the golden curtain still glittered in the Highland light, they made me very welcome with drinks on the terrace of their idyllic lochside house, with what must be one of the most sensational views in all the Highlands: south across a small inlet from Loch Alsh to the wooded shores of the peninsula with no name and up to the bare peaks of Kintail beyond. This landscape reflected the sinking sun as the four of us sipped our G&Ts and caught up with news of friends old and new.

I'd first met the Sage several years before, when visiting him with a mutual friend, whom for our purposes I'll call the Wanderer. At that time he'd just moved into a village some way up the coast from here and on the first day, while the Sage went out to work and the Wanderer looked up old acquaintances, I was left in charge of the house, with a few tasks to keep me occupied. One of these was to call at the local newsagent's where the Sage had just set up an order for his regular periodicals. The doorbell rang as I entered.

'Good morning. Mr MacKillop's *Times Literary Supplement*, please.'

(The name and details are not the real ones.)

'Are you Mr MacKillop?' enquired the elderly shopkeeper.

'No, I'm staying with him. He asked me to collect it.'

'But Mr MacKillop said he'd be calling for it.'

'Oh, well he won't be here in the daytime till Saturday.'

'I can only give it to Mr MacKillop. Are you Mr MacKillop?'

'No.'

'MacKillop's a new customer. Ah canna give his papers to just anyone!'

'No. Well, never mind, then.'

He gave me a mischievous glance.

'Are you *sure* you're no' Mr MacKillop?'

'Er, well, I could be, I suppose.'

'Ah, Mr MacKillop! Welcome to Balanish!' grinned my interrogator and handed me the journal.

That evening, the Sage, the Wanderer and I walked round to the local pub where I'd lunched alone, they with their instrument cases all ready for the evening's 'session'. The landlord greeted me like a long-lost friend.

'Ah, Mr MacKillop, your friends can play then?'

'No, no, I'm not…' I thought I'd lunched incognito but had evidently underestimated the speed at which local news could travel, even the wrong news.

'What'll you have, lads? On the house! Any friend o' Mr MacKillop's a friend of oors.'

Well, by the end of the evening our real credentials had been established. Many pubs in these parts host regular 'sessions', where the musicians sit and play traditional tunes in a corner, welcoming any newcomers but not necessarily dominating the other customers. In the Celtic tradition, all the music is unamplified, of course, and not really 'for show', but essentially for the musicians' own pleasure. The Wanderer plays guitar and pipes, while the Sage plays a mean fiddle. Looking rather sheepishly at my free ale, I played only with my beer mat.

Since that visit, the Sage had changed jobs, moved house again and married. Both he and Rosemary tend to meet many people from the local communities through their work and lead what, to me, seems an unnervingly hectic life at odds with this peaceful part of the world.

After the second G&T, I started dipping into their local knowledge base. What had I missed by not coming via the Kylerhea ferry and Màm Ratagan?

'Oh, just some of the most spectacular scenery in the Highlands, Richard,' said the Sage. 'The pass is at about a thousand feet and gives you spectacular views over the Five Sisters.'

'Which five sisters?'

'The Five Sisters of Kintail, man – those five peaks there.' He gestured over his shoulder, not needing to look at the view that greeted them every morning.

'You also missed the chance of a cuppa at the Jac-O-Bite,' pointed out Rosemary.

'Oh, that awful name!' groaned the Sage.

'Talking of names,' I said, pointing across Loch Alsh, 'what's the name of this peninsula here?'

'Oh...' hesitated the Sage.

'Knoydart?' suggested his daughter.

'No, that's farther south, um...'

Well, for once the Sage was un-sagelike and they had to accept my proposal of Dunnodart. They did, however, know where the action was in Lochalsh that night. After eating, we were to go to a Mull Theatre production in Kyle and after that, to the session at their local in Dornie.

'The Shinty Boys'll be appearing there,' said the Sage's daughter.

'I don't think I've heard them,' I said.

'*Heard* them?'

'I don't think I've heard them play.'

'You don't hear them, Richard,' corrected the Sage, 'you *watch* them. They don't play music, they play the game.'

'What game?'

'Shinty, man! They're the shinty boys!'

My woeful lack of Highland knowledge was addressed for a few minutes more, including the revelation that the tall goalposts had been on a shinty pitch, not a football pitch, until the evening's schedule had me rushing through the shower to get ready. I quickly gathered that this session with 'the shinty boys' would not be a gentle exchange of tunes but a raucous exchange of rounds of ale.

A man's game

At school in England in the 1960s, we thought shinty was just a scaled-down version of the girls' game of hockey. How wrong could we be? Shinty is a hard man's game played widely in its traditional core area, the Gaelic heartland of the Scottish Highlands. (I hadn't even known it was Scottish – whoops!)

In Gaelic it's called *camanachd* and the Camanachd Association points out that 'its demands of skill, speed, stamina and courage make *camanachd*, the sport of the curved stick, the perfect exercise of a warrior people'. An ancient sport, its rules were eventually codified in 1879. In essence it's a twelve-against-twelve stick-and-ball game with no kicking and with ball-handling only by the goalie, who may, say the rules, 'slap it or stop it with his open hand'. Rather you than me, mate.

Shinty is taken very seriously up here, although, as with all sports, it's the comradeship among the teams that's even stronger than the rivalry between them.

At the time I was in Lochalsh, Fort William were top of the Marine Harvest Premier League. Local side Kinlochshiel were having a good season near the top of Division One North and that Saturday had clocked up a 2–0 away victory against Skye.

The play by Mull Theatre was excellent. I'm not a very arty person and was therefore a little apprehensive about a play called *Art*, but this tale of friendships battered by the controversial purchase of a completely blank white canvas was extremely funny, well performed and professionally produced. For all this, though, the laughter and applause at the Kyle Village Hall were rather sparse, for the simple reason that the four of us from Avernish accounted for nearly twenty per cent of the audience. Rosemary, who helps put on these and many other local events, confirmed that a great deal of work is involved in getting them together. Indeed, on my route here I'd seen many posters advertising this very production. Come to think of it, though, with Kyle's total population being only 739 – and let's say twice that in the overall catchment area – the hit rate was about 1.75 per cent, which in the small Leicestershire borough where I live would bring nearly 3,000 spilling through the turnstiles. A fantastic turnout for *Art*, then!

En route back, I was actually quite relieved when, instead of a session under the table with the shinty boys, we opted for a session under the stars with the Merlot boys (and girls). And what stars! It was a while since I'd seen the night sky away from street lights and I don't think I'd ever seen it quite as stunning as this. From a back garden in the Highlands on a cloudless, moonless night, we were treated to not only the raw, ragged arc of the Milky Way, but also the recent phenomenon of a 'moving star' that is really a man-made satellite (the multinational Space Station), and a more traditional 'shooting star' – first one, then another and then yet another: 'Ooh, that one went on for ages!'

After a while I noticed a cloud advancing from the north and thought the display was soon to be over, but the Sage's experience kept us observing the 'cloud', which turned out to be no such thing but rather the 'aurora borealis', the Northern Lights, something I'd been longing to see ever since I was a boy. It appeared as a glowing brightness on the northern horizon where no town stood to confuse us with its street lights. Many stars were still visible through the violet-white glow, which curved and wavered before our eyes.

Being a teacher, the Sage was just the man for the moment, reminding us what we were actually looking at. Each 'shooting star' was a piece of speeding grit colliding at high altitude with the earth's atmosphere and burning up in the heat from friction. The 'Milky Way' was a sideways-on view of the billions of worlds in our own galaxy. And the 'Northern Lights' are the result of high-energy, charged particles from the sun interacting with the earth's magnetic field and striking the gases of the ionosphere, causing them to glow, just as a fluorescent light tube: different colours for different gases, violet for nitrogen. The Sage himself had once been lucky enough to see the full 'waving curtain' effect and told us how easy it must have been for the ancients – and maybe the not-so-ancients – to see messages from Heaven in these patterns drawn in the sky. This was the best light show on earth and it's always free. The others stayed out for more, but my cycling neck was 'giving me gyp', to use the phrase my Uncle Harold favoured to describe his aches and pains, and I retired to my bed where, for once, I think I literally did fall asleep before my head hit the pillow.

Chapter 9

Back on Track: Lochalsh and Loch Carron

An unhurried day for a change. Unhurried breakfast and unhurried farewell to the Sage and his family. So why did I forget my exercises? As a youth I'd just jump on my bike and be off, but some eight years earlier on a charity bike ride across Cuba, I'd joined in the stretching exercises insisted upon by our leaders every morning, often before a crowd of giggling Cubans peeking around their doorways. With about eighty Europeans of all ages, shapes and sizes togged up in multicoloured Lycra, I think anyone can imagine the gigglesworth of the sight. Anyway, we did all get from one side of Cuba to the other in one piece, which seemed remarkable enough to suggest the stretching worked and so I've done it before bike rides ever since... until this Highland morning that saw me gaily pedalling along the shores of Loch Alsh, obliviously unstretched.

I was, however, somewhat inspired by having been allowed to touch the hallowed wheels of a famous bicycle in the Sage's shed. One morning in the strike-torn days of the 1970s, an eighteen-year-old Junior Sage found himself stranded in Aberdeen with a long-planned Continental holiday due to start the next week – but separated from his target by a strike-bound British Rail network. Not one to be bullied by the workers, he simply (simply! ha!!) jumped on his drop-handlebar Raleigh and pointed south. Five days later and the boy was shaking his fist in triumph at the Thames Estuary. Makes my fifty-mile days look pretty puny, doesn't it? Mind you, he was going downhill.

With my task put in severe perspective, I shot off by the banks of Avernish, the very banks on which a local dignitary sadly met his death during one of the many battles over Eilean Donan Castle, just around the corner on Loch Duich. The reason I bring this briefly to your attention is for you to relish his name: the poor man was Donald Gorm MacDonald, fifth Baron of Sleat.

If you turn right at the main road, you enter beautiful Kintail, where *The Statistical Accounts of Scotland* tell us that in 1836 'in a population of 1,240 souls, there is only one drunkard'. No name and address provided. However, returning to my west coast route after the long

Adnamurchan and non-Knoydart detours, I turned left and back into Lochalsh.

Much of this small peninsula is occupied by the Balmacara Estate, run by the National Trust for Scotland, theoretically with the aim of encouraging traditional crofting (working rented smallholdings) but to all appearances with the aim of getting visitors out of their cars and wandering around the native woodlands and pretty little villages that dot the peninsula. And good luck to the Trust with that. Just past Reraig I dived left down a track towards the shore to pass through the estate's 'woodland garden' with its ferns, hydrangeas, rhododendrons and bamboo, all combining to deaden the sound of the A87 and redirect your attention to a little beach with views across the sparkling morning waters to the deserted shores of Skye. This diversion also reinforced The Rule, of course.

Holding to the mainland in Kyle, I pedalled past the Mull Theatre's blue van parked outside a B&B and up onto the heathland that looks north over the mouth of Loch Carron to the barren wilderness of Applecross. Well, pedalled only so far before walking and then walking only so far before groaning, cursing and parking Tetley at a bench while I belatedly did my stretching exercises. Unusually, I had a passing audience as this bright Sunday morning had brought out several fit-looking walkers, one coughing smoker, a heavily laden blackberry-picker and, of all things, two cyclists.

As you emerge onto the tops here, you're treated to views over Drumbuie, Duirnish and Loch Carron that must must rank among the best in the Highlands, even when accompanied on this occasion by banks of threatening cloud tumbling in over the peaks above the village of Lochcarron. At Duirnish I dipped left again, partly to follow The Rule through the little hamlet but also to have a coffee break by the gurgling stream that divides the two rows of houses. A 1970s guide by the Wester Ross Tourist Organisation stressed the pleasure of escaping here from the hurly-burly of the modern world. As the Sage and Rosemary had shown me, though, if you happen to live here it turns out to be even more of a hurly-burly than in the city, for the simple reason that a good proportion of the people you pass in the street are likely to know you and want to buttonhole you about the local church fete. If either of them had been sitting on this rock, they'd doubtless have been whisked inside for a gossip, while I, the visitor, could idly stare into the little stream for as long as I liked. So I did.

For too long. A glance at the watch revealed I was behind schedule, partly because of my late exercising, on what was supposed to be an easy day. No time for Plockton, then. The village that sounds like it's been transplanted from a sleepy little hollow in Devon is the most picturesque around here, so that its palm trees and loch view feature on many a box of Highland shortbread. With its sheltered aspect (hence the palm trees), two excellent pubs and an aerodrome to boot, it's also at the peak of local property prices and on a walk along Plockton's 'prom' you may struggle to hear any local accent. Or, as the road sign clumsily puts it: 'Plockton. Scotland's Best Village for Tourism.' By the way, the name's an anglicisation of *am ploc*, the promontory.

My route took me along another steep, single-track road up onto the heath again where it was almost blocked by seven shaggy Highland cattle gathered for a Sunday morning horn-wag. Leaving the stranded occupants of a Renault Mégane wondering how to get past, Tetley and I sneaked around the blindside and pedalled on. A cascade of ferns tumbled down the hillside to the left before a rapid descent took me back into the bosom of a dark, leafy wood where yet more rhododendrons lurked behind long, neat drystone walls. With each bend I expected a sign to announce: 'Lochalsh Hall. Home of the Dukes of Lochalsh for six centuries. Uninvited callers will be shot and eaten'; but none did. What did arrive, though, announced by a heavy tap-tap-tippety-tap on the broad leaves of the undergrowth, was rain – the first since Glenborrodale, three days ago.

It was sudden and it was sharp. I stopped at a convenient bus shelter to don my not-very-waterproof jacket, and then again half a mile later at a less convenient lay-by to don the not-very-waterproof trousers that I'd forgotten. I was already half-drenched and wondered if the occupants of the Dutch motorhome by which I was changing might invite me in to the dry, but no such luck – probably afraid I'd steal their chocolate sprinkles.

By now I was back on the main road and passing 'Stromeferry – No Ferry', as the sign calls it. 'Strome' comes not from Gaelic but from the Norse *straumr* (current) and reminds us that, as you go north from Kyle, you begin to enter the area of Scotland occupied for many years by the Vikings, whose longboats swept in from the Minch. There once was a ferry across Loch Carron from here over to

Strome Castle, a fifteenth-century fortified tower, guarding the entrance to the loch and which had been destroyed as usual in a long-gone tribal conflict. The ferry service stopped in 1873 when the road around the head of the loch was built. By this time, the Highland Railway from Inverness via Dingwall had already reached Stromeferry, but it wasn't until 1897 that the difficult westward extension to Kyle was finally opened, starting a boom period for Kyle as the railway and ferry terminus.

Beyond Stromeferry a '14 per cent' sign soon saw me pushing Tetley up a long, steep hill. I've never really got the percentage method into my head in the same way that the old '1-in-5' method was embedded and find that I have to divide it into 100 to get a picture of the gradient. I know that 1-in-10 isn't too bad, while 1-in-5 is something to remember. So it seemed a good opportunity to use the creaking of the neck and the pinging of the calves to impress upon me what 14 per cent meant. Another distraction was to address myself once again to the impossibility – for surely that's what it was – of pushing this same weight up the formidable 600-metre pass that would be the defining feature of the next stint.

Fortunately I'd got about six months to work on this, as Stage 2 was about to end. My target for today was the 15.59 ScotRail train at Strathcarron station, which would quickly whisk me to Inverness and thence, care of Virgin Trains, back to England and the pressing needs of a normal twenty-first-century life.

The rain eased before I reached Strathcarron to reveal a sprinkling of snow on Glas Ben beyond the north shore of the loch. The Sage and Rosemary had already told me that food would be available at the Strathcarron Hotel and so I was pleased to have at least some of the planned hour to spare before my train was due. After quickly stripping off my yellows and locking Tetley to the drainpipe, I eagerly left the rainy day outside and entered the pub. It was like entering a time capsule. It looked like Led Zeppelin had played here in 1976 and never left. The bar was hidden by a forest of denim, leather, greasy hair and shaggy beards. Some of the blokes looked a bit rough, too. Squeezing my Lycra cycling shorts through the denim hedge, I ordered a burger and chips. One of the bar-flies spoke:

'Ah dinna know 'bout yiew, but ah'm still f**kin' steamin'!'

'Yes, lovely day, though,' I ventured, quickly retreating with my coffee to a distant, dark corner.

As I munched hungrily on the burger, a young man who wouldn't have been born when Led Zeppelin were around stumbled through the door with first one, then two, then two more enormous loudspeakers. This was followed by yet more equipment, more cables and a single electric guitar. The room where he set up this equipment was half-filled by it and I wondered, as I had many times before, what the actual point of amplification in a small room could be.

Happy to be outside in the rain again before the afternoon session began, I walked Tetley over to the station. Also boarding the little diesel unit that now works this, the furthest north of the lines that reach out to Scotland's wild west coast, were two of Led Zep's groupies: one with black boots, torn tights and bright pink hair, the other with big heels, torn denims and bright green hair. Both were singing. Still steamin'?

Metaphorically steaming back to reality, I reviewed my progress. On the positive side, I was over halfway to Cape Wrath with all my limbs still functioning. On the negative side, I really needed to resolve the issue of the combined weight of the bike and me — and resolve it fast, as the journey's biggest challenge would face me on the first day of my return.

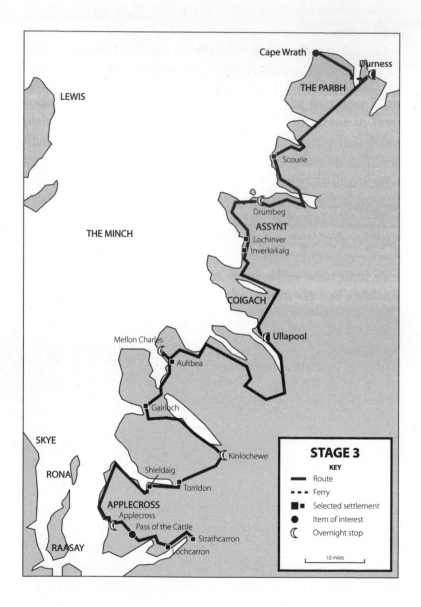

Cape Wrath

Durness

THE PARBH

LEWIS

Scourie

Drumbeg

THE MINCH

ASSYNT

Lochinver

Inverkirkaig

COIGACH

Ullapool

Mellon Charles

Aultbea

Gairloch

Kinlochewe

SKYE

Shieldaig

RONA

Torridon

APPLECROSS

Applecross

Pass of the Cattle

Strathcarron

RAASAY

Lochcarron

STAGE 3

KEY

── Route

- - - Ferry

■▪ Selected settlement

● Item of interest

☾ Overnight stop

10 miles

Chapter 10

The Sprightly Reverend and the Porridge Drawer: Applecross

Nine months had passed since that rainy September day and it was an early July day that threatened more of the same as we pushed off from the station car park. Yes, we. Putting his bike clips where his mouth was, the Sage had committed himself to a day and a half accompanying me at the start of this, the last stage of the trip.

Despite shedding a few pounds, I'd decided that the weight issue needed a more drastic solution. Tetley's load had been made substantially lighter than on the nine preceding days by the exclusion of all my overnight gear, for I'd recruited a support car, crewed by my partner Julie – plus, as long as the Sage was my co-rider, by Rosemary too. The riders would leave the support team early each morning and we would meet up again each evening. The first night's accommodation was pre-booked, but choosing it for subsequent days would be Julie's main job, the choice being communicated to me by mobile phone. Not every middle-aged adventurer is lucky enough to have Julie's enthusiasm and organisational skills to call on. So as the Sage and I pedalled off from Strathcarron station, the support team was still back at base in Avernish.

It had been an extraordinary weather year so far for Britain, with June turning up in April and April in June – twenty successive showery days having preceded my departure from the English Midlands and hundreds of Yorkshire folk still evacuated from their flooded homes. You may remember it. No surprise, then, that I'd togged up that morning fearing the worst. Some small surprise, though, to have seen the Sage preparing his own cycling gear that morning: a tall, neat man bending over the ironing board to prepare a crisp blue cotton shirt before squatting on the floor to polish his cycling shoes, a rather smart, brown leather pair that would not have seemed out of place on a senior stockbroker's feet. Indeed, when saddled up and on the road, the Sage did look rather like a stockbroker who had agreed to undertake a charity bike ride and now regretted not having simply put the money in the tin instead.

Reminding myself that this was the man who'd pedalled his Raleigh from northern Scotland to southern England in five days, I followed the leather shoes along the short run around the loch head to the village of Lochcarron. In doing this, we were leaving the relatively bustling central portion of the west coast, stretching from Loch Linnhe to Loch Carron, with its plentiful road and rail links to the Central Lowlands. From this point, we were creeping ever further into the far north-west, which I felt sure would mirror the remote feel of Kintyre and Knapdale in the far south-west. We were entering MacKenzie territory and pushing further into Wester Ross, part of the former county of Ross and Cromarty and, before that, of Rossshire – famous for its magnificent scenery and for its even more magnificent triple S.

Lochcarron, a long, straggly but very pleasing settlement of nearly 1,000 people, had been a tiny village called Janetown until the road from Inverness reached here in 1813. From then until the 1970s this formed the main road west to Kyle, via the ferry at Stromeferry, but another new road, completed in 1973 along the southern shore of the loch, made the stretch south of Lochcarron village something of a backwater – in fact a dead end, which is why our route skipped it and headed west over a range of low hills down to Loch Kishorn.

Travelling here with the Sage was like travelling with a local celebrity:

'Hi there!'

'Hello yoursel'!'

'A fine bike that, mon!'

At the Kishorn Seafood Bar, even the tale of my own heroic journey was cut short by the latest gossip to be shared between the friendly assistant and the Lad Himself. Rather ominously, this included the tale of a recent cyclist's heart attack up on the Bealach na Bà, 'The Pass of the Cattle', our route to Applecross. Let's hope it wasn't set to be renamed 'The Pass of the Doomed Cyclists'.

Notwithstanding this latest news, the KSB's excellent coffee and scones provided just the boost we needed for the assault to come and it was still with confidence that we emerged, though under ever-darkening skies. While the Sage dived into the wee shop opposite to buy a vital piece of equipment he'd forgotten (this turned out to be a comb), several heavy, wet drops through the slits of my helmet prompted me to pull on more waterproofs. The Met Office's weather forecast for the area this week had been oddly phrased: 'While there is some possibility of an occasional dry spell between the showers, there is low confidence in this.' Surely showers *without* dry spells would be just rain, I thought. Oblivious both to such niceties and to the rain itself, the Sage emerged fully equipped for the office at last and, as the leather shoes pedalled off to the north, I squished in place behind them.

Loch Kishorn looks small, picturesque and empty now but, strange to tell, it was here in 1978 that human beings constructed the largest movable object on earth. 'Ninian Central' may sound like a stop on the Cardiff metro, but is in fact a 600,000-tonne oil platform still working in the North Sea and was built at Howard Doris's Kishorn Yard, which completely dominated this corner of the Highlands for twelve years in the 1970s and 1980s. Three thousand workers hammered and riveted their days away on this little loch and – I know you're thinking this – where did they all live? Answer: on two retired ocean liners moored out in the loch. Obvious, really.

Just after three British-registered motorbikes thundered close by our right ears, we turned left off the A896 to be greeted by a barrage of red warning signs that did their best to discourage the unwary from the road ahead and encourage them back onto the more sensible route to Applecross via Shieldaig. Dismissing such defeatist signage, the Sage and I breezed straight past these warnings to take the challenge on the chinstrap. The unnumbered single-track road over The Pass of the Cattle is the third highest in Britain, rising from sea level to 626 metres in about six miles, but apparently the only one which learner drivers are officially dissuaded from even attempting. Before it was surfaced, and without the alternative coastal route around the north of the peninsula, which was completed only in 1976, access to Applecross and its neighbouring settlements was normally by sea. Except, it seems, for cattle, which were evidently deemed too heavy or costly for the craft of the time and therefore driven over the pass that bears their name. The 1937 Ward Lock guide called it simply 'a steep way for wheels', and it still is.

Shortly after the gradient commenced I replaced happy breezing with heavy breathing as I settled into a steady push mode. As I approached the Sage, who was to spend the next two and a half hours alternately pushing on ahead and then waiting for his older companion to catch up, he called:

'Come on, man, the ascent hasn't started yet!'

It's all right for you in your ironed shirt, mate. The rain had stopped by now, the sky was lightening and I relieved myself of a protective layer or two while the Sage pointed out items of interest in the slowly widening view. Across the loch odd white bits of Plockton village had emerged between the islets that protect it. To the left stood Duncraig Castle, made famous a few years before in the TV series *The Dobsons of Duncraig*, featuring its purchase by an extended Leicestershire family and the typical televisual shenanigans that followed. To the right, Plockton's little airfield and short stretches of the Dingwall-to-Kyle railway line. I'm afraid I was paying less attention to the Sage's lessons than to recovering my breath. Onward and upward.

(Amazingly that short shower proved to be the last actual rain to fall en route for the next seven days. The continuing downpours and floods in England at the same time were, it seemed, due to the jet stream having temporarily shifted south this year. England was the new Scotland.)

Turning one more corner, we were hit straight between the eyes by a view of the challenge that lay ahead. Filling the horizon was a complete semi-circle of glowering, grey-green Tolkienesque mountains, the tops of which were hidden by a continuous ragged, cloudy fringe. Our road zigged and zagged into the centre of this amphitheatre, eventually forming the merest thread of silver until, just near the edge of a giant grey ledge, it disappeared completely into the distant blackness.

Well, we pushed and we stopped and there was a short lesson from the Sage; push, stop, lesson; push, stop, lesson... I learned that the Bealach, whose gradients rise to 20 per cent, was also featured in *Hamish Macbeth*, that it forms part of several cycling events, including a ninety-mile race in which the winner shot up the Bealach in 36 minutes, and that the Sage had wanted to tackle it for years. Occasionally, for a bit of variety, the Sage actually pedalled a little before stopping. For my part, I just pushed and stopped. For long stretches nothing but our own feet and breath was to be heard. No wildlife seemed to live in this dark and gloomy corner of the Highlands. No rustles in the heather, no birdsong.

Two German motorcyclists overtook us at a sedate speed, turning to offer a sympathetic grin. A descending black Mercedes stopped to wait for me to pass, its driver winding the window down to impart in a broad Yorkshire accent:

'Seventy miles to go yet, lad!'

Ah, that legendary Yorkshire humour. 'Lad', though: that was encouraging.

As we got higher, the temperature got lower and a gulp of still-warm coffee was welcome to us both. Even the Sage's lessons were showing signs of wear and tear.

'This bowl, er... phfff... this corrie, classic glace... phfff... glacial scenery.'

'Yes, phfff, geographer myself.'

'Ah yes. Phfff. Onward and... hhoowah... upward.'

About an hour and a half after the start of the climb we pushed over the edge of the ledge, from where the view of the stretch we'd just climbed had already disappeared. A gushing waterfall thundered over in the opposite direction. Our narrow road teased us by first flattening out a little before lurching into a series of precipitous hairpins that pinged the calves and reduced my own progress from strides to mere steps. After another half-hour or so, the Scottish driver of a muddy Land Rover en route to Kishorn gave me the good news:

'Dig in, boy, you'rrre nearrrly therrre.'

'Boy'! As the air got thinner, I must have been getting younger – or deafer, perhaps.

Eventually, having lost sight of the Sage for the previous ten minutes, I rounded another bend to find him disrobing at a bench beside a clutch of parked cars and before a new and dramatic view to the west, a view that Groome's team had described 125 years earlier as being 'as savage and sublime as Glencoe'. The top. The Bealach was beaten.

Just as I pantingly pushed Tetley over to the bench, the beeping of a newly arrived car had me turning to see two familiar faces grinning through the windscreen of a golden Toyota: the support team. General hugs, kisses, handshakes and congratulations. Pop bottles, Marmite buns and photos. Mopped brows, shared tales and, of course, lessons.

Julie and I are both rather short and, though considerably older than the Sage, stood as two schoolchildren paying close attention to their master's words. Rosemary, rather too tall to be one of the pupils, stood a little way away; perhaps she'd heard the lesson before.

'That's Raasay and that's Scalpay. And in and out of the cloud that's Pabay. Or is it one of the Crowlin Islands?' The Sage's geography was being severely challenged by a herd of shifting cloudlets. 'But those are definitely the Cuillins. And there, look,' he continued as a gap of brightness spread, 'there, above Skye and beyond the Sound of Sleat, is the

Ardnamurchan peninsula.' From our high vantage point, it all appeared in exceptional 3D.

The support team soon retreated to the car from the clammy cold of summer on the Bealach and I too was keen to feel the inside of a warm room. So, agreeing to meet up at the Applecross Inn, the Golden Toyota drifted off on its descent, followed closely – rather more closely than I'd expected – by two speeding cyclists.

With a 30-mph wind chill to add to the cold afternoon, it was a really bitter as well as exhilarating descent. When, at a halfway plateau, I pulled up by the Sage's side, my ungloved fingers were already turning blue and my toes numbingly humming. The Sage's office gear seemed to be coping better than my own cycling gear as he pointed to the desolate plain below.

'No vineyards there,' he declared, and with that enigmatic truism pedalled off again, only to stop within a minute as a corrie opened up to our right.

'And that,' he declared, translating from the map, 'is the Corrie of the Flies.' We both stared into the grey-greenness for swarms of midges or clegs but saw none, nor any reason for their proliferation here. Absence did not make the heart grow fonder of the pests and we pushed off again… or rather pulled off, as the bikes hurled themselves down and down and down until the Applecross shore halted our juddering slalom.

The six-mile climb had taken two and a half hours; the six-mile descent a mere 25 minutes; reconnecting my fingers and toes to the rest of my nervous system another two and a half hours.

★

The Applecross Inn, being so remote and isolated, was the only overnight we'd booked in advance and I'd been anticipating this evening for weeks, even months. As we'd saunter into the quiet, low-lit bar, the weather-beaten faces of the only other customers — old fishermen Angus and Hamish — would rise in gruff welcome from their misty beers, anticipating rare news from the outside world. What was this new-fangled wireless machine? Was the Suez Crisis over yet? Who was this Presley character who so excited the youngsters? Maybe they'd call down to old Florrie in the kitchen to bring up some haggis and gruel for the weirdly dressed strangers just blown in from the land beyond the Bealach.

Slightly off beam. In fact a quick calculation using the Scale of Remoteness (see Chapter 3) showed that in Applecross R = 1, a very low score indeed.

The little hotel was full, despite the pricey room tag. The restaurant had would-be diners hovering keenly for a free table. The bar itself was tightly packed, for the most part with confident young things whose BMWs, Porsches and Range Rovers were pulled up outside by the Applecross strand. The usual cocktail of West Highland languages could be overheard: German, French, Polish, Spanish, a muttering unintelligible to me that could have been Russian or Portuguese — and English. One or two Scots claimed the strip of bar nearest the ale pumps but their accents were more Hamilton than Highland and their language English — well, Scots English. I may as well tell you now that in my entire journey from one end of the Highlands to the other, during which I was privy from my bicycle to more snippets of wayside conversation than I'd care for, I heard not a single word of Gaelic.

The Gaelic name for this area, *a'Chomraich*, means 'the Sanctuary', but 'Applecross' is a corruption of *'aber crossan'*, mouth of the River Crossan. It's believed that this western shore of the peninsula has been settled from, rather incredibly, about 6000 BC, that being the date put on a midden (a domestic waste area) found just north of here at Sand. At the Applecross campsite, just inland from the inn, is the site of a broch (an Iron Age roundhouse) built between 200 BC and AD 100 and confirmed as such by a very wet Tony Robinson and his Channel 4 *Time Team* chums. Next up was another Irish Christian, St Maelrubha, who settled here in the seventh century. Say what you like about these Christian missionaries, they certainly had an eye for a pretty spot. It's a shame that St Maelrubha's name has failed to drift down the centuries as easily as St Paul's or St James's, denying us the pleasure of meeting a Maelrubha MacKenzie or perhaps buying a single by Little Maelrubha Osmond. Maybe there was a Maelrubha MacKenzie, for it was in support of the MacKenzies' Applecross Estate, and their grand eighteenth-century Applecross House a mile north of the inn, that the village developed.

The settlement straggles along the shore for half a mile to the south and the Sage, the support team and I took a pre-dinner stroll down here to gaze across to Skye and the silver curtains of rain rushing across its mountains. Actually, I was also gazing in hope of spotting a clifftop home that had been described to me over a year before.

*

At the very start of this trip, on my way to Kintyre on the Ardrossan–Arran ferry, I'd met up with another cyclist, the only other on the boat and about the same vintage as me. He rode an old, heavily pockmarked, drop-handlebar job, with a traditional, hard-leather Brooks saddle. With my brand new machine, front suspension and squishy saddle I felt a bit of a sissy, but, when we got talking about our trips, I was quietly confident about the manly challenge I'd taken on.

'Where are you off to?' he asked.

'The Mull of Kintyre,' I answered breezily.

'Then where?'

'Oh,' I said, trying to let the low morning light catch my rugged jaw, 'Cape Wrath, actually.'

'Uhuh.' I'd been expecting at least a 'Wow!'

'What about you?' I asked.

'Oh, John o'Groats,' he countered.

'Wow! When do you expect to be there?'

'Um, let's see. Sunday night probably.' It was then Friday morning.

'The Sunday after next?'

'No, this Sunday.'

Well, that shut me up, didn't it?

He was an English vicar and an end-to-ender, i.e. someone propelling himself between Land's End and John o'Groats under his own steam. There are thousands of them, it turns out – walkers, runners, cyclists, pea-pushers (who knows?) – along with their end-to-end records, their end-to-end websites, their end-to-end heroes and all the other paraphernalia of a cult. The shortest end-to-end route is about 840 miles and has been cycled in under two days, allegedly – I assume by Clark Kent with a following wind. However, one of the end-to-enders' guidebooks (Paul Salter, *Bike Britain*) says encouragingly that the more usual 950-mile route can easily be cycled in about three weeks. At 45 miles on just an average day, this is a usage of 'easily' that's new to me.

Many of the cyclists used to swish past the Sprightly Reverend's house and, as middle age approached, he'd decided that if he didn't do it soon himself, he never would. After clocking up what seemed to me like phenomenal daily mileages (the previous day he'd charged the hundred-plus miles from Carlisle to Ardrossan), he now had the Groats firmly in his sights.

He was a skilled DIYer too. While I can just about understand how a bike works, I make a point of never interfering with any moving parts, lest I break them. The Sprightly Reverend was of the opposite persuasion. He outlined to me the major en-route repairs to his old machine, including repeatedly having to knock his wheels back into a vaguely circular shape after some mishap or other. He was a walking toolkit. When he moved, he rattled.

On arrival in Brodick, on Arran, he soon rattled past me and by the time I'd wheezed into Lochranza just in time for the ferry over to Kintyre, he'd not only had a tour of the village and a snack at the cafe, but also made a running repair to their toilet's leaking cistern. God's works evidently include plumbing.

By the time we split up at Claonaig on Kintyre, he'd told me about his family's second home at Applecross. It had been a complete ruin on a clifftop, with no electricity, no road, nor even a track. No problem to the walking toolkit, though. He and his family brought all their building materials in by boat, lugging them up to the ruin and transforming it into what sounded to me like a paradise on earth. But it wasn't just the description of his home on the cliffs that came back to my mind as the four of us strolled by the sea. It was his tale of the porridge drawer.

When breakfasting with an Applecross family some time ago, the Sprightly Reverend had been offered some porridge by the lady of the house.

'Oh, yes please,' replied the Rev.

At which she pulled open the drawer of a cabinet and, brandishing a large knife, enquired: 'One slice or two?'

And there before him was a drawer-shaped mass of porridge. Solid porridge. Apparently it was a local custom to make porridge by the giant panful and then pour it into a drawer lined with greaseproof paper, there to cool and solidify until required, at which time – I assume – it would be quickly warmed up again, slice by slice, in a pan. Now, it's just possible that the Sprightly Reverend was taking spanner number six to wind me up something rotten, but now that I was finally in Applecross, the authenticity of the local porridge drawer was something I was keen to nail down.

Slotting into our reserved table among the multitude at the inn, I intended to raise this question with the local landlord, but his northern English accent dissuaded me. Maybe the waitress at breakfast.

Chapter 11

The Dolt and the Sage: Applecross, Torridon and Wester Ross

The next day did not start smoothly. My little blue bag of spare cycling equipment had gone missing. While the Sage was with me, we could share his emergency kit, but from that afternoon I'd be on my own again, as he and Rosemary would leave us at Shieldaig, where their car had been left. If everything went well, I could carry on with no problem, but if anything went less than well – for example, if my bike got a p... p... you know, the P word – then I'd be... you know, the F word, as my scheduling didn't include much time for contingencies.

The others must have been annoyed, but were all skilled at hiding it. It was generally agreed that I must have left the little blue bag at Avernish and therefore breakfast turned into a logistical summit focusing on how best to get the bag and its hapless owner reunited. The only solution seemed to be that, after the Sage and Rosemary had returned home, one of them would drive back with the bag and meet Julie halfway. The Sage had been looking at the neat fold-out map from my 1937 *Ward Lock Illustrated Guide Books: The Highlands of Scotland* and, noting how little had changed in the last seventy years, scanned it in search of the best handover point. While he was puzzling, Rosemary, efficient as usual, had already worked out that it was Achnasheen.

For my part I was still distracted by my embarrassment at having caused this chaos when the waitress arrived for the toast order, and I ordered mine as 'untoasted toast', confusing the North American girl until the Sage stepped in:

'Around here,' he translated, 'we call untoasted toast "bread".'

With my stock already low, I proceeded to sink it further by converting this bread into sandwiches for later in the day – an act that, judging from the frowns around the table, broke the basic etiquette of the formal Scottish breakfast. When, after returning to our room, I was compelled to report the remarkable discovery of the little blue bag right there inside the big blue bag, where it had been all the time, my stock fell yet further. Moreover, the lack of local staff had meant the question of the porridge drawer had to remain unanswered yet again.

Departure from the Applecross Inn was thus a muted affair. It's not that I didn't accept fully my idiocy, but rather that we couldn't settle on a word for it. Over the first few miles northward, full and open discussion on the topic with the Sage lightened things a little: was I merely a fool or a twazzock? Perhaps an idiot or even an eejit? It soon became apparent from such pondering on the myriad ways of folly that this was very much an area of specialised knowledge and interest on the part of the Sage. There was no stopping him: pillock, halfwit, moron, numbskull, plonker, buffoon…. Eventually, although the local term 'barmpot' briefly held sway, we settled on a very short and very precise description of my shortcomings: I was simply a dolt.

Relieved that the matter was settled, I began to take in my surroundings. Today's weather was perfect for cycling: cool, dry, overcast and with a following wind. With the Inner Sound (formerly the Applecross Sound) as our constant companion, we positively breezed north along the 'new' coast road. Except, of course, when the Sage stopped for an impromptu lesson. His stops seemed to bear no relation to the dynamics of cycling. As usual he'd be several hundred metres ahead and I'd be catching up via a top-gear charge, when his stationary, pointing form had me losing all momentum as I screeched to a brake-block-burning halt.

'What?'

'There's a castle over there somewhere.'

'Where?'

'On Raasay.'

'Where?'

'I can't see it.'

(So why did you stop, oh Sage?)

'Onward then?'

'Right.'

The Sage's lessons today seemed to have morphed into constant searches for the invisible, even the unknowable. As we drew level with Raasay's northern neighbour Rona, the Sage once again stood at a gradiently inappropriate spot and pointed out to sea. Pulling to another fist-clenching halt, I peered where he pointed.

'What?'

'You can sometimes see submarines on naval exercises near Rona.'

'Can you today?'

'No.'

'Oh.'

'Onward?'

'Onward.'

Actually, the Isle of Raasay itself, with its protruding volcanic peak of Dun Caan, looked remarkably like an enormous submarine but, as official Dolt of the Day, I kept this observation to myself.

A century ago the small island of Rona supported a resident population of 161. According to information available at the time of writing, the island's population is now 1. His name is Bill and he sits on a hill... Well, actually his name *is* Bill but he sits in his lodge as the caretaker of the Isle of Rona Holiday Cottages. This isn't the first time on this journey that a dramatic reduction in the local population has been mentioned – and it won't be the last. Time, I think, to confirm why this is so.

Canada or nowt

We studied the nineteenth century at school in the 1960s. Oh yes, we learned that George Stephenson's 'Rocket' won the Rainhill Trials in 1829, that Victoria became queen in 1837 and that Prussia won the Franco-Prussian War in 1871. Nobody thought to mention that in a corner of our own country over half a million people were forced to leave their homes to make way for sheep and that there are now more descendants of these people living abroad than there are in Britain.

The Highland Clearances just didn't appear on the radar of English school history. Even when I first read about them, as a twentieth-century townie I didn't quite see the problem: if your landlord gives you notice to quit, you scour the classifieds for another pad. However, there was no such thing as 'cosy, two-bed flat, loch view, convenient for spade shop', and no *Highland Evening Standard* to spot it in. Moreover, the Clearances were too often a matter of life and death and unsurprisingly were all down to money.

By the eighteenth century, wool was big business in Britain and the development of breeds of sheep that could be reared easily in mountainous terrain like the Highlands meant that the region became one big business opportunity. Some of the estates were huge and the connections, whether geographical or social, between landowner and tenant were often remote. By the early nineteenth century, the 'improvements' being instigated by many landowners, to replace arable with pastoral farming, meant quite simply the forced removal of the tenants – along with the destruction of their homes to prevent any return. A little different from the termination of a contract on an apartment in Notting Hill.

'Opportunities' for the displaced families were often on the coast, where the land was even less suitable for farming than inland and where in any case they would have had to build a new home before even thinking about growing food to eat in it. An alternative theoretically on offer was fishing – but you try starting a dangerous new profession from scratch without a government-sponsored training scheme. And even if these activities were feasible for some, they were impossible for the large numbers being turfed off the land. Often enough, then, it was Canada or nowt.

Although the immediate effect was the sudden depopulation of the Highlands, a later one has been the apparent transformation of surviving crofters (the tenant farmers of the Highlands) from victims to heroes, as successive governments have given them more rights than you can shake a rake at. Nowadays, apparently, to benefit from the support available to crofters, the definition of crofting has been widened a little from the traditional scraping of a living from the soil, to include cleaning, caretaking, driving a bus and even working on the Web.

The very next settlement on our route, Lonbain, is yet another victim of the Clearances, with a whole abandoned village street being clearly visible to anyone willing to leave the road. Which we weren't. With the freshening wind at our backs there was no stopping the Sage and me... until he spotted something else missing, of course.

In sharp contrast to the east (Bealach) side of Applecross, this side of the peninsula was alive with the flashes of tiny skitting birds, the twitter of their calls and the rapid changes in light that passing skies brought to the landscape. Around Callakille a herd of seven or eight deer trundled across the road and then, as the more alert among them saw us coming, clattered more urgently up into the heather, over a ridge and was gone. Just as fast to come and go were many of the vehicles parked up at the inn the previous evening: the usual German, French and Dutch plus a fair spattering of Danish, Norwegian and Swiss. One common factor was that none contained children – July must be prime holiday month for child-free Continentals to escape before the family hordes clog up Europe's roads in August. At other points in the next few days I was to spot Czechs, Hungarians, Austrians, Rumanians and even a vehicle from the Faroe Islands ('FO', car-spotters). The West Highlands must be on the twenty-first-century's Grand Tour.

Out to the left, Rona's lighthouse emerged and, beyond that, the vertical cliffs of Skye's Trotternish peninsula, looking like an upturned beer crate dropped into the sea. Beyond that a low island off Skye was the last land to be seen, much to the Sage's disappointment – for there he was, true to form, scanning the nothingness of the north-west horizon.

'Lewis is there,' he stated, pointing Lewis-wards, but Lewis remained very much hidden in the cloudy haze.

By the time we reached the corner of the peninsula at Fearnmore, a new landscape had opened up and we both stopped to gaze at the many fingers and arms of the mainland to the north, distinguishable only by their different shades of grey. The Sage had driven this way before.

'You can see the next few days of your route here, Richard. Beyond Redpoint – there, you can see the orange sand – beyond there in the distance are the Gairloch peninsulas, possibly Rubha Mòr and almost certainly those furthest peaks are Coigach.'

'You've been to all of them?'

'Just about. But I haven't spent enough time anywhere up here. Boy, I certainly envy you this trip.'

'I'm just passing through, though. The schedule doesn't include much time for hanging around.'

'But you're retired.'

'Retirement doesn't remove all your responsibilities.'

'It'd remove a hell of a lot of mine!'

'You've years to go, mate. Don't wish your life away.'

The Sage looked out over the green, rolling landscape again. In addition to features that were visible, he focused on one that was stubbornly not so. He was gazing at the orange expanse of Redpoint beach.

'There's a youth hostel over there.'

'Where?'

'Don't know. Can't see it. Can you?'

'No.'

'Oh.'

'Onward?'

In turning the corner, we'd not only changed our maritime partner from the Inner Sound to Loch Torridon but had also passed a more significant – and, for a change, very visible – boundary. As highlighted at Loch Linnhe, the landscape of the southern Highlands – lochs, mountain ranges, headlands – is orientated south-west to north-east. From this point it shifts to being north-west to south-east. Look at any map of Scotland and you'll see that the Applecross peninsula is the changeover point. Loch Torridon, together with its northern neighbours Maree, Ewe, Fionn, Broom, etc., all the way up to Cape Wrath, take a south-easterly bite into the mainland. One of the reasons I'd chosen to do this trip south to north rather than north to south was to benefit from the help of the prevailing winds, including this morning's breeze-powered charge up the coast. So it was with confidence that I predicted to the Sage a tougher regime from here on in.

I was wrong. Ducking and diving down through Fearnbeg, Kenmore and the other tiny settlements that gazed across the loch to Ben Alligin, we still seemed to have the wind behind us. Feeling thus charmed, but short of someone else to talk to, we pulled in at the first brown tourist sign: 'Stained Glass Workshop. Visitors Welcome. Open.' By the time the Sage had removed his helmet, combed his hair and smoothed down today's fresh pink cotton shirt, I'd established that this was in fact 'Stained Glass Workshop. Visitors Barked at by Dog. Closed and Locked.'

Re-emerging on the road, we bumped into the support team on their way round the peninsula – after all, there's only one road. We were just in time to share an extraordinary view down in the loch: four or five large compounds in which the surface of the water seemed alive with the effects of a localised underwater earthquake. A closer look through the support team's binoculars revealed the cause to be hundreds of wildly jumping fish apparently intent on escaping from a fish farm. Having each had a look, we agreed to meet up in Shieldaig (with the support team, not the fish).

Over the neck of a small headland at Ardheslaig, we descended to the shores of Loch Shieldaig, the second loch in the new orientation, and to tantalising glimpses of the small white village of Shieldaig itself, sheltering under the mass of its mountain. More and grander peaks, Liathach and Ben Eighe, loomed behind, heralding the giants of the North-West Highlands that would be present for the rest of this trip.

After taunting us from across the water, Shieldaig finally yielded to our wheels and the two brave boys careered into town to cheers from the team. This was a bit surprising, as we'd wondered if they'd be sitting in the pub grumbling about hanging around for the 'boys'. It's not a bad spot to hang around in, though. Shieldaig's a pretty little place, perched at the water's edge but sheltered by its own tree-covered island. In 1800 the British government set up the village as a training ground for seamen to serve in the Napoleonic Wars. Now, I don't know much about naval warfare, but a single village in Rossshire doesn't sound like a large-scale commitment to me. I understand the Brits won, though, otherwise you'd be reading this in French. (Perhaps you are.)

It was here that riders and support team were both to shrink by half, as the Sage and Rosemary returned to the real world – a reluctant return in the Sage's case, as he pedalled up and down the seafront searching in vain for an excuse to carry on. Farewells were shared and, in my case, promises given to continue my regular wayside lessons alone. As I pushed my way back up to the main road, the Golden Toyota — now just with its one-woman support team — waved encouragement and headed off in search of tonight's digs.

My lochside company had changed too, this time to Upper Loch Torridon, with Ben Alligin looming left, Ben Damh looming right and straight ahead the highest of them all around here, the 1,053-metre massif of Liathach, doing a super-loom that shrank the straggly settlement of Torridon at its foot to a string of maggots. The hamlet of Balgy came and went without a Sage to tell me what it meant but, with the sun breaking through at last, I cheered myself up with a quick burst of 'I'm awaaaa the noooo' to an audience of three black-headed gulls that squeaked in protest. Incidentally, I've since done my homework and discovered that in the phrase I'd shamelessly lifted from stereotypical Scots, 'the noo' does indeed mean 'right now'. Maybe everyone else knew that.

Torridon was known as Fasag until 1950 (why do these Highland villages keep changing their names?), but whatever its name it looked a miserable sort of a place and I passed it by. Fairweather, however, (for we continue to pedal in his wheeltracks) turned left through Torridon for the hazardous haul over the cliff-and-beach track up to Redpoint, some sixteen miles distant. As much of this is apparently uncyclable and includes crossing a stream with no bridge, The Rule didn't require me to take it and so Julie and I had earlier agreed to meet up in Kinlochewe, from where she'd already called with the good news that a bed was organised.

The road along Glen Torridon looked straight and easy on the map and, for once, it proved actually even easier than I'd thought, as not only was the breeze miraculously still at my tail but also the glen quickly assumed the sort of gradual downhill gradient that touring cyclists crave and confirmed the Fourth Law of Cycle Touring: that wind and gradient are effectively the same thing. In this case they combined to shrink my effort and I was able to freewheel for several miles, sitting up straight to take in the stunning scenery.

Liathach and Ben Eighe bustle so closely to the road here that at times it seems they're going to eat it up. Their overwhelming presence is eased slightly by their oddly light grey tops formed from white quartzite. What surprised me most, though, was that through much of the glen someone had scaled these mighty flanks to place regular lengths of fencing that formed giant rectangles on the mountainside, as if to say 'Man was here'. I guess they're to keep the sheep in.

Among others impressed by the grandeur of this area was that irrepressible fan of Scotland, Queen Victoria, who, one day in 1877, was happily making some sketches around here when the comment of a passing American perplexed her somewhat. He gave the opinion that the area was 'very ugly' and that he was thus hastening south to England. Yep, baffles me too, Vic. In pretty short order I was wheeling into Kinlochewe (the 'ewe' is pronounced like the sheep, i.e. 'yoo') and turning right at the Kinlochewe Hotel to dismount after an excellent day's cycling. The excellence didn't stop there. All the hotels and guest houses at which I – or now, we – overnighted on this trip were independently owned. Whether the tedious hotel chains of England can't be bothered to invest in the Highlands of Scotland I don't know, but their absence is surely to the guests' benefit. The Kinlochewe is a hotel with a history, having been host more than once to the Scottish Mountaineering Club in the days of the renowned Munro, after whom the Munros are named. To prove the fact, photographs of the man himself, as well as his colleague Corbett, are amongst those taken outside the hotel in 1899 and 1928 and on display in the bar.

We learned this over an after-dinner glass of wine with the owners, a half-Scottish, half-English couple, who had only recently taken over the hotel. We were sitting in their comfortable lounge-cum-library as they relaxed after a long day. Both of them had the facility, once having been 'switched on', of launching themselves through one subject after another in a stream-of-consciousness kind of way without any further outside intervention. The key decisions on taking over a rather run-down hotel, we learned, were in allocating the priorities.

'Where do you think we've spent the money so far?' we were asked.

Plenty of opportunity for a faux pas here, I thought.

'Well, the towels look new,' ventured Julie, to encouraging nods, 'and the soap's certainly not a bulk buy from Boots.'

'No indeed,' confirmed the landlady, 'it's handmade in a little studio up in Mellon Charles.' This was near our route for the next day and Julie noted the details.

'But you'll have noticed the decoration's still pretty grim,' admitted the landlord. 'You know, we slept in each room in turn ourselves to see what guests would need doing most.'

'I'd never have thought of that,' I said.

'It's the only way to do it. But most of the money's gone elsewhere...' He lay back in the generous armchair and stretched his legs, still covered in a chef's striped apron, and gave me an enquiring look.

'Ah, well,' I suggested. 'We've just had an excellent meal, of course. Um, a new kitchen?'

'And the rest! The whole bar and dining area's new.'

'Yes, of course,' we both assured him. 'It's beautiful.'

'You've got to keep your regulars and pull in a few more if you can. The bar's the top priority. It's your bread and butter.'

Well, after a few more tips on how to 'pull them in', including the success of a Hallowe'en fancy dress party and regular 'vinyl nights', we departed not only well fed and well watered, but well instructed on how to make a success of the hotel trade. To be honest, Julie and I had often agreed that it's one of the last jobs we'd ever take on, knowing that while we looked forward to a long night's rest, others would be locking up late and getting up early to keep the business going.

Mind you, with my current trip explained to them, our hosts were convinced it was me who was mad.

Chapter 12

The Dining Room That Time Forgot: Lochs Maree, Gairloch and Ewe

Glimpses of blue sky sent me off in good spirits the following morning and the scenery soon improved them further. The A832 from Kinlochewe to Gairloch follows the southern shore of Loch Maree and glimpses of its deep-blue surface between the shining stands of silver birch kept me company for several miles. The 'Undiscovered Scotland' website rates Loch Maree as 'a very strong contender for the title of Scotland's most scenic loch'. I'm never very sure about lists of most scenic this and most beautiful that as so much depends on the day, the season and the beholder; but I wasn't going to disagree this morning.

This particularly deep loch has over twenty islands, all officially administered as Sites of Special Scientific Interest on behalf of their owners, although I'm struggling to think what 'administration' an uninhabited island may need: permission for a tree to grow, perhaps? In fact they weren't always uninhabited, for some incomers not only lived but also died here. Royalty actually, for Prince Olaf Haafager, son of King Haakon of Norway, was buried on one of the islands in 1137. This reminded me that the further north I travelled along this coast, the less the influence of the Gaels that blew in from the south and the greater the influence of the Vikings that blew in from the north.

What's the difference between a Viking and a Norseman?

'Norse' is the generic term for the people of southern and central Scandinavia up to the eleventh century. A Viking is simply a Norseman on the move, and the move from the end of the eighth century was an aggressive one on much of Northern Europe. Viking longboats were way ahead of other contemporary vessels and, specifically, the addition of a keel meant that they could carry many more warriors than before.

The Norsemen first took Shetland, Orkney and Caithness – probably with little opposition, as these were sparsely populated at the time – but when they reached Cape Wrath and began to press southwards, they met with more resistance and things got nasty. In three invasions of Iona from 794, the Vikings destroyed Columba's abbey and killed 68 monks.

They inflicted such a complete defeat on the Picts that the latter's kingdom fell into the hands of the Scots of Dalriada. Following these Viking raids, Norse settlers colonised the Hebrides and much of the mainland's western seaboard, creating a north-western kingdom, Sudreyjar, over which the Scots had no control.

Now, you're expecting me to say that the Norse influence is still noticeable in the local place names, aren't you? It turns out, however, that the Scots, under Malcolm II, regained control in the nick of time (early eleventh century), so that the *skagis*, *strönds* and *víks* (capes, beaches and bays) of the Norsemen could be happily Gaelicised again before being safely anglicised a few more centuries down the line.

The exceptions, those place names deriving clearly from the Norse, are mostly way off our route in Caithness, Orkney and Shetland, the islands remaining Norse for another 400 years. The Norse Earls of Orkney, by the way, went by some fabulous names. Thorfinn the Mighty (1020–65) was preceded by Sigurd the Stout, who was preceded by Thorfinn Skullsplitter. 'I was thinking of asking the Skullsplitters round to lunch, dear – what do you think?'

The opposite shore, partly wooded and partly bare rock, tumbled precipitously from the 990-metre Slioch ('the spear') into Loch Maree, but the track along it used to be the main route south for market-bound cattle drovers from Poolewe on the coast. Further along that shore, Letterewe (which could, I suppose, be spelt 'U') was the site of a seventeenth-century iron-smelting industry fuelled by charcoal from the local forests and using iron ore from England, which was the cheaper to transport. Much of the local woodland was felled and, after 300 years of recovery, was felled again during World War II to make ammunition boxes.

After a few miles of nothing but trees and lake to the right and marshland and mountains to the left, the smells and sounds of a farmyard suddenly heralded a clutch of buildings at Talladale, followed closely by the small but perfectly formed Loch Maree Hotel by the lakeside. Here I pulled in to sit on the verge for a sip of coffee and a change of map. All the way from the Mull I'd been using sheets from a 1:200,000 OS map tucked into the top of my bike bag, but for some reason this morning I'd switched to a 1:50,000. It was a mistake. Even at my slow pace, cycling is too fast for this large scale and has you stopping to turn the map over at annoying intervals. Having returned to the good old 1:200,000, I pushed off, now with Gairloch at least in my map's sights.

Before anything but tarmac was in my eyes' sights, it was to be a long haul up a featureless slope. Not audibly featureless, though. While still not far from the lochside I could hear a louder than usual torrent draining the hillsides to the left. I hope Queen Victoria was impressed. These Victoria Falls were named after you-know-who to commemorate her 1877 visit. But there's a very strange bit of geography here – and a spot of intrigue to boot. The local dignitaries didn't think the flow over the falls impressive enough for Her Maj and so, being Victorians, they just tinkered about with nature, by diverting part of a stream up in Flowerdale Forest until they'd pumped up the volume to meet royal requirements. 'Part of a stream?' Surely you either divert a stream or you don't. Well, actually, no – they did exactly what they said they'd do, leaving a fascinating phenomenon up there on the tops, where the River Loch na h-Oidhche now splits in two, half flowing west to Loch Ewe and the other half east to Loch Maree. Is there nothing those Victorians couldn't do? Their queen surely should have been impressed.

Having reached the top of the slope, I remounted and pedalled into what was a completely different landscape. The parallel loch and mountain ranges had now disappeared to give way to a new hummocky terrain, orientated left–right and with narrow white tracks tracing erratic patterns across its surface. On one of these, in the middle distance, bobbled a red, a blue and a yellow cagoule, presumably with humans inside them.

A stiff breeze had appeared from nowhere to make progress difficult and when, just by the roadside and at the head of a little lochan, a small wooden shelter appeared, I took the hint and scuttled into it for lunch. The back wall of the hut was entirely covered by a map telling me that the hut, the map, the paths and bridges were all provided by the Gairloch Estate. A hastily typed note pinned to the bottom told me further that a good many of the bridges had recently been washed away by storm-filled torrents. The estate had also provided a large, smooth stone on the floor of the shelter on which I placed my padded bottom while snaffling the Marmite sandwiches prepared at breakfast. Just in time, as it happened, for my stay in the shelter was brought to an abrupt close by the arrival of a heavily equipped German couple who needed to scrutinise the map before commencing their route march across the hills. Tetley and I gathered our bits and pieces together and were on our way.

The main loch in the Gairloch Estate, bearing the glorious name Loch Bad an Sgalaig ('loch of the bad slag'?), emptied into the River Kerry, which paralleled my road down to the coast. Given the recent bad weather and the full loch, it was odd that the riverbed carried only a trickle of water and I puzzled over this until seeing the large green pipeline zigzagging down the valley beside me and eventually the small hydroelectric power station where it ended. Below the station the river resumed its natural strength and tumbled through a peculiarly luxuriant valley, looking more Devon than Dingwall.

Gairloch is an oddly unsatisfactory sort of place. Yes, it has a busy little jetty, a great beach (with this journey's first sunbathers), an impressive-looking hotel, a comprehensive grocery store (though its Eastie assistant called me 'Dear'), a friendly little bucket-and-spade shop and an eminently browsable bookshop-cum-coffee bar. The unexpected problem is that it's a stiff walk for the tourist between each of them – and there was also something else off-putting that I couldn't quite put my finger on.

At the far end of this straggly strand I met up with Julie for lunch at the Mountain Coffee Company cafe for an excellent vegetable soup and a quick loan of George Hendry's book *Midges in Scotland*. This classic volume is recommended for anyone planning a summertime visit to the West Highlands and a quick flick through taught me yet another thing I hadn't known about these pests: that the darker the sky the more likely they are to come out and get you. So on a bright day they come out later, on a dull day earlier.

Having agreed with Julie an approximate zone for this evening's sojourn, I left her with a sudoku to resume my uphill pushes on the steep route out of Gairloch to the north. Looking back, I realised now what else was wrong with the place. Having secured the standard Highland coastal site of sheltered bay among looming hills, the city fathers had failed to install the requisite row of whitewashed, eighteenth-century, single-storey terraced houses down on the seafront. Goodness, if you want to cash in on the tourists you really do need to plan 250 years ahead.

Ascent into the wild country was sudden. The pattern that unites this whole route is a continual switching between high, wild country (95 per cent of the terrain I crossed) and low, sheltered coves (the other 5 per cent), where almost all of the civilisation lies. The laws of physics, at least the laws of bicycle physics, mean that the descents are usually rapid and exhilarating, the ascents slow and painful. For some reason, the ascent out of Gairloch surprised me in its speed. It also surprised Tetley's cogs as the chain shot off them all and left me pedalling thin air. A displaced chain is about the only cycle repair I can achieve in less than 24 hours but this one was closely observed by a persistent wasp whose grasp of the English language – at least the two words of it that I repeatedly directed its way – was shaky.

So it was with oily hands and a bruised temper that I resumed my progress across the neck of Gairloch's peninsula. The pesky wasp wasn't the only reason. I'd called at Gairloch's tourist information office to pick up the phone number for the next day's ferry across Loch Broom from a dot on the map called Allt na h-Airbhe, that would give me a free afternoon in Ullapool, one of my favourite spots on the west coast. The officer-in-residence had retained her fixed smile as she revealed that the chap who ran it had given up a couple of years ago. Tomorrow's schedule was suddenly looking stretched.

My cloudy mood, though, was soon lightened when a sudden and unexpected view opened up to the south. I thought I'd bid farewell to Loch Maree but the bend in the A832 just above Poolewe had several cars, including my first Hungarian spot, braking to an injudicious halt as Maree's long blue waters stretched out to the east below the tumbling green slopes of the Letterewe Forest.

Another squeaky descent dropped me at the mouth of the short River Ewe that drains Loch Maree into the sea at Poolewe. Yes, I know the Marmalade Theory of Highland Place Names predicts that this little village should be called Inverewe ('mouth of the Ewe'), but then until 1700 Loch Maree used to be called Loch Ewe, now the name of Poolewe's sea loch... so it's pretty confusing around here already. For my afternoon break, Poolewe offered me pizzas and Highlandburgers one way or a bench overlooking a beleaguered angler with a Range Rover the other. Making fun of the fisherman got my vote.

While I just about see the pleasure of standing in a metre of cold rushing water wearing thigh-high boots, I've never seen the point of bothering the stream's resident wildlife at the same time. This young man, who lost his footing every time he cast the line, had about as much chance of catching a fish as hooking a harvest moon and when a salmon (I assume) jumped out of the water in front of me, heading in the opposite direction to its would-be tormentor, I pointed, shouted 'Salmon!' and laughed out loud. Crassly unsympathetic we townies, aren't we?

Cheered by the incompetence of one of the shunting and hooting set, I set off up the eastern shores of Loch Ewe. During World War II, Loch Ewe was used as a strategic assembly point for the Arctic convoys – merchant ships on the dangerous 1,600-mile route to Murmansk, to supply the Russian front. On one of these runs the on-board contingent included my father, which is odd as he was in the army and had no experience of the sea. As I passed a set of moss-covered gun emplacements at Tournaig, I wished I'd asked him why.

Soon after, pulling in at a lay-by for another break, I was taken aback by the view in both directions. Behind was spread a panorama of the Torridon Mountains and other peaks that I thought I'd left behind over a day ago, while in front lay a new, sparkling blue expanse of eastern Loch Ewe, with at its centre the cutely named Isle of Ewe. (Why this hasn't yet been developed as a prime honeymoon destination I don't know.) Beyond spread the green slopes of the Rubha Mòr peninsula, spattered with an astonishing number of scattered white dwellings.

Julie had already checked in at one of these, Mrs Mac's guest house at Mellon Charles, and when I cruised down past Aultbea's NATO fuel store she pulled alongside to offer me a lift (Julie, not Mrs Mac). Mellon Charles was at the dead end of a road deemed unnecessary by The Rule, you see, but the softly mellowing afternoon had raised my spirits still further and so, gracefully turning down the offer, I pressed my knees into a further five miles of service.

Aultbea was one of the Allies' main deep-water anchorages during the war and, judging from the plentiful information boards that drew my attention, had become a pretty serious naval base by the end of it. Today, it housed just a small fishing fleet and a large coastguard vessel moored out in the loch. As I was wondering what employment might be available around here nowadays, I rounded a corner to be faced by a small gang of youths whose only current employment seemed to be sitting on the kerb. Their jeers as I approached suggested I might be their only potential victim of the day and so I shouted:

'Hey, lads, is this the way to Glasgow?'

This was clearly the funniest thing they'd heard since England got knocked out of the World Cup – except for one lad, who charged up to my bike, waved a manic fist very close to its rear wheel and yelled:

'New baik! New baik!'

Taking this to be a traditional Highland welcome, I grinned as I sped away and was soon garaging Tetley outside the neat white lochside house of Mrs Mac at Mellon Charles.

★

Everything about this Mrs Mac, her house and her garden was neat. Exceedingly, fanatically, hysterically neat. Quite a lot of it was blue, too. Our bedroom had a blue carpet, blue wallpaper, blue duvet cover, lampshades, curtains and cushions. If Julie had worn a blue dress and Venetian face mask she'd have completely disappeared.

One of Mrs M's conditions for accepting our booking was that we'd be in the dining room for tea at 6.30 p.m. sharp. I made sure I'd washed behind my ears too, just in case. At 6.29 p.m., along with one other couple, we assembled in the dining room where the friendly pair from Stevenage indicated which of the three tables was ours. At 6.31 p.m., Mrs Mac (I assume it was her – for she spoke not a word, neither of introduction nor explanation) entered from the kitchen with two plates of piping hot asparagus soup for the Stevenages; at 6.32 p.m. she served us ours; at 6.34 p.m. she poked a steel-lipped face around the door as a family of three occupied the third table and, at 6.34½ p.m. served them their soup, by now evidently at least half a degree below the specified temperature.

The dinner – which I should say was delicious in every way – continued with similar military precision, as plates were silently removed and replaced, cutlery was neatly stacked and whisked away and cups and glasses were carefully placed in their allotted locations. At one point I tried to strike up a conversation with the Stevenages, but it died away in the muffling silence created by Mrs Mac's intensely disciplined routine. I strongly suspect that she's a mainstay of the Mellon Charles Line Dancing Club.

The room in which we dined was decorated in eerily precise deference to 1970s suburban chic. Shiningly polished display cabinets bore symmetrical arrays of gold-edged plates, delicate pink jugs and miniature china figures depicting parasol-toting ladies and chest-puffing matadors.

The only slightly dissonant note came from a row of replica racing cars on top of the dresser, but even these were in alphabetical order from Benetton to Williams.

The only point at which we diners had any choice in our fare was when coffee and After Eights (seven mints for seven guests) were served in the lounge: we could either take them or leave them. Happily taking them, we had a brief conversation with the Stevenages about their 'new town' that is no longer really that and then emerged into the happy chaos of the countryside for a stroll in the mellow gold of a perfect July evening. The walk took us past 'The Perfume Studio', the source of the previous night's handmade soap and around which Julie had made a brief tour earlier. It was certainly an idyllic spot for any business.

Being so far north, the evening light lingered later and later and the whole landscape was still washed in a golden glow at midnight. On another occasion we may have made use of Mrs Mac's terrace until the small hours, but the next day was due to be the longest since Ardnamurchan and the blue bed in the blue room called...

Chapter 13

Destitution Road: Gruinard Bay and Lochs Broom (Little and Large)

After twelve cycling days of incident and interest (except perhaps for the sodden haul from Kilmartin to Oban), the thirteenth, from Mellon Charles to Ullapool, was dull indeed.

It wasn't just the lack of a Loch Broom ferry and the consequent 44-mile slog via Destitution Road; nor the grizzle – grim, grey drizzle – that had replaced last night's sweet sunset; nor the lack of a single bus shelter or even a bench; nor the mile after mile of undulating terrain with more pushing than pedalling; nor the lack of a single signpost in the first 32 miles by which to monitor my progress; nor the lack of interesting features about me (unless you count the distant view of an anthrax-plagued island interesting); nor the repetitive emergence of identikit grey headlands to the north. It was all of these things combined.

Pushing up the hill away from Aultbea, where I'd rejoined the main road, I had to admit that someone else had already had a worse day, as I tiptoed around the entrails of a dead sheep, the carcass of which was both mourned by the baaing lamb behind the fence and closely observed by the two gulls on it.

At least the mist kept me cool and, remounting at the top of the hill, I was able to benefit from its refreshing touch as I freewheeled through Laide and turned right along the southern shore of Gruinard Bay. When I pass place names by the roadside, I often wonder who chose them and under what circumstances. The next two baffled me, though. It was undeniable that this was a coast road, but couldn't they have come up with something better than 'First Coast' and 'Second Coast'? Maybe the anonymous place-namer had also found themselves on a dull, misty day with a long haul ahead. At the next little spot, it seems they glanced to the left to catch a view of a yellow-grey strip between the brown-grey track and the blue-grey loch and, with a flash of creativity, called it 'Sand'.

Rounding a bend and climbing up a little rise, I was surprised to see in a lay-by a young man with a ponytail and a single earring setting up his professional-looking camera on a large tripod and pointing it at... at what? You may well ask. I pulled up and stood in line behind his viewpoint. All I could see was a mud-coloured bit of sea, a grim piece of Gruinard Island and the endless cover of flat, featureless sky. And yet he started snapping away at it. If I were you, I'd look out for calendars entitled 'Grey Bits of Scotland' and 'Places to Avoid in the Highlands'.

The day was encapsulated by my lunchtime soup stop. Like London buses, there were no cafes on this stretch for many miles until three arrived together near Dundonnell. Pulling in at the first, clattering Tetley against an outside table and then dragging off my sweaty, sodden kit inside, I looked around. Despite my jolly 'Hellooo!', the tightly-coiffed assistant kept her head down; two sombre middle-aged couples sipped sombre coffee on sombre tartan benches; one ponytailed spinster examined the tea towels, unable to decide between the Castles of Scotland and the Clans of the Highlands; the CD rack consisted entirely of a preselected set of 'ambient' Scottish and Irish music; and, of these, I'm pretty sure it was an endless spool of Clannad that was gumming up our ears. Add to this the view of a light grey mist hanging over a dark brown loch and you'll recognise the joint as a standard Celtic Suicide Cafe. They start at Gretna and end... I don't know, maybe here.

Even the historical tales along this stretch share doom as their theme but, held to them by a kind of morbid fascination, I'll recount them anyway.

The anthrax island is Gruinard Island, set in Gruinard Bay. In 1942 it was used by the British government for experiments in germ warfare (so don't go claiming that it's only the baddies who do that kind of thing), wherein anthrax was disseminated on the island, wiping out its flock of sheep. Gruinard was immediately placed in quarantine, a status destined to last 48 years. In 1986, at a cost of half a million pounds, the island was eventually decontaminated, a procedure that involved removing all the topsoil in sealed containers. By 1990, sufficient tests had been undertaken for it to be officially declared safe and Gruinard Island was sold back to the owners from whom it had been compulsorily purchased during the war – and for the same price, £500. The film of the scientists' work remained classified until 1997.

From my lunch stop the road climbed up through the wooded valley of Strath Beag for about five miles before emerging to cross a bleak expanse of open moorland, on which a sea of dark green, hummocky grass was split by a network of small streams whose busy work I could hear every time I stopped. This stretch of the A832 over the pass between Dundonnell and Braemore Junction (with the A835) is called Destitution Road, as it was built to provide employment after the 1851 potato famine, another disaster on which many history books have been silent.

Another clear-out

The huge impact of the Irish Potato Famine of 1845–9 is well documented – deaths, destitution, emigration – but the fact that the same potato blight also hit the Scottish Highlands is rather less well known. At least, it was to me. The crofters who managed to remain on the land after the Clearances had much less territory by which to sustain themselves than before and the potato was the one crop that had some chance of feeding their families from such small acreages. However, in 1846 a fungal disease blighted the crop and, following a particularly cold winter in 1846/7, there were signs of famine similar to the Irish famine of the previous year.

For whatever reason, though, a relief operation was put into action more quickly and with more effectiveness here than in Ireland. Oatmeal and other supplies were distributed by naval vessels (under the command of the unfortunately named Sir Edward Pine-Coffin). Crop failures continued into the 1850s and, though relief supplies also continued, the recipients were expected to work for them in some way and building the so-called 'destitution roads' was one form of payment.

Some landlords were keen simply to remove the 'troublesome' crofting tenants from their lands and more evictions followed in the wake of this agrarian crisis, just as in the Clearances. Between 1847 and 1857, by which time the potato crop had recovered, 16,000 Highland crofters were shipped to Canada and Australia.

The long haul over the pass did have the bonus of taking me past wild Fain and the Fannichs — I'd buy their first album (no doubt called *Destitution Road*) just on the name of the band. Fain is a remote, windswept house while the Fannichs, sometimes known as the 'Rossshire Alps', are the mountains to the south-east.

Spilling out at Braemore Junction definitely felt like being back on a beaten track and the hint of sun on distant Loch Broom further lifted my spirits — as did the first sight of Ullapool a few miles later and then the happy sighting of a red CalMac funnel after a few more. The A835 carries most of the traffic to the North-West Highlands from Inverness and was the first primary route I'd followed on this stage, which is why it took me a while to stop waving at each vehicle that passed. After the bleakness of the preceding six hours, this was a pleasant stint between steep stands of conifers to the right and some patches of mixed woodland to the left, beyond which the quiet waters of the loch eventually came into view.

'Broom' comes from the Gaelic *bhraoin*, meaning 'place of rain showers'. Though there are wetter places in Scotland, the rain seems to suit Ullapool's character, as this poem written by the Wanderer confirms:

Ullapool: *Nach Bog An Latha?*★

Damp. The mist over Ulla's pool slides down the raised beach to mix phases with the sea loch.
Damp. The heavens weep tiers of tears. They shudder down to mix phases with the mist.
Damp. The frost on Ulla's pool trembles; it hesitates to free the blunted grass blades.
Half-heartedly, grudgingly, it mixes phases with the rain and mist.
Damp. *Nach bog an latha?*

★ Isn't it mild?

Ullapool was living up to this reputation by the time I quickly de-biked behind the convenient quayside guest house discovered by Julie. I was fortunate to have such a well-organised partner as a volunteer one-woman support team on this last stage. On business trips, Julie had often stayed in luxurious accommodation throughout Europe, North America and the Far East, but like me, also appreciates the quirky places that meet a quite different market. She found plenty on this trip.

Like the Mrs Mac's of the previous night, this one was caught in a time warp, but rather by lack of attention than surfeit of it. Old-fashioned, stick-out light switches, rickety mirrors, broken door handles and flowery duvet covers (two on one bed, strangely) all conspired to convince you that, bar five minutes from a daily cleaner, no one had ventured in our room since 1975. I wouldn't have been surprised to come across a Bay City Rollers LP in the wardrobe. Another twenty years and Tony Robinson's chums will be digging a trench across the bathroom.

I like Ullapool. It has that frontier feel of wild country being all around but good tucker being available within. We took our tucker at the FBI, where I'd once stayed on my only other tour of the north-west nearly twenty years before. In Ullapool, FBI means Ferry Boat Inn and, in our case, FCB meant Fish, Chips and Beer – a choice that also seemed popular among the Poles, Germans and Americans that formed the bulk of the FBI's clientele.

Ullapool is one of those settlements where the name comes not from Gaelic but from Norse: *Ulla-Bolstadr* meaning 'Ulla's farmstead', the Vikings having arrived here at the end of the eighth century. Americans should feel at home here now as today's Ullapool was a planned settlement complete with its grid pattern of streets, albeit only a four-by-four grid. But the town was built not by farmers or gold prospectors but by, of all people, Thomas Telford for the British Fisheries Society in 1788. Shoals of herring out in the Minch had already been a rich source of food for local fishermen before the town was laid out and the earlier fishermen's cottages are still there on the shore, some even still homes, squashed among the tea rooms and gift shops tempting the tourists with their sticky corn flake cakes and tartan shawls. Ullapool is a popular stop on the Highland coach route and every summer day sees the town's population dramatically expanded by the arrival of retirees from south of the border... including ourselves.

The whitewashed new town was built to service a boom in herring sales but, with overfishing and the decline of stocks, this was eventually over by 1900, leaving a tidy town struggling to survive. To the rescue, however, came not only tourism but also a new generation of long-distance fishing vessels, as well as about sixty 'factory ships' from the USSR and other Eastern bloc countries in the Cold War days of the 1970s, whose job was to process mackerel caught by smaller vessels.

Even though its resident population is now only about 1,200, Ullapool is the only place of any size on the last stage of this trip and also the last Caledonian MacBrayne ferry terminal, with its service to Stornoway on the Isle of Lewis. When the ferry pulls alongside, its red-topped presence easily dominates this little lochside town.

When Francis's team documented Ullapool in 1891, 2,043 of its 2,096 population were Gaelic-speaking. Groome also commented that 'Ullapool is well suited to be a noble watering-place, its beach being capital bathing ground [and] its climate pleasant and salubrious' (*Ordnance Gazetteer of Scotland*).

I suppose drizzle could be salubrious.

Chapter 14

Serious Cases of Remotitis: Coigach and Assynt

The youthful energy of a teenage boy in green running gear was undimmed by the drizzly weather as, the next morning, I assiduously followed The Rule by leaving Ullapool via its neat back streets which were the closest to the loch. Emerging on the main road again, I followed a sign reminding me that I was leaving the last place of any size on my route: it pointed left and said simply 'North'.

At the top of the long drag out of town a glance over my shoulder revealed the bright red of the Stornoway ferry just pulling away from the quay and so I quickly remounted to catch up with it on the other side of a small headland. Such is the speed of the vessel, though, that by the time I got there it was already chugging out into the Minch and almost out of sight.

From here the only road turns inland and during the long pull up Strath Canaird the Highland drizzle became more persistent but couldn't quite be bothered to turn into actual Highland rain. Eventually, as I turned left at Drumrunie into the heart of Coigach on an unnumbered single-track road that would feel my wheels for the best part of the day, it was neither drizzling nor raining; it was draining. It was draining at the turn and it drained all the way along the banks of Loch Lurgainn. I could tell that this would be a sensational route if you could actually see anything through the drain. Indeed, the tourism people had placed many a well-produced information board detailing the geological importance of the dramatic scenery I couldn't see. The Sage could well have written them.

Let's not allow my misfortune to stop me trying to summarise what the boards were on about...

Crunch time

Part of those dramatic goings-on around 400 million years ago that created the general north-east/south-west 'grain' of what is now western Scotland was a 'thrust fault' in which some older rocks were forced upwards and westwards to lie over younger ones.

This event is called the Moine Thrust and, being contrary to what you may reasonably expect – that newer rocks would overlay older ones – it confused the hell out of Victorian geologists. The place where the evidence is most clearly laid out is Knockan Crag and the chaps who solved the mystery were Ben Peach and John Horne, revealing to the world for the first time the possibility of huge geological forces taking place over long periods of time.

The A835, which I'd just left, more or less follows the line of the Moine Thrust and also runs past the Knockan Crag Visitor Centre where, should visitors be lucky enough to see further than their windscreens, they can observe exactly what Peach, Horne and their buddies got so excited about.

The road through Coigach would be (and perhaps is) an ideal stretch along which to test any new gear system in any vehicle: for about twenty miles you shift from top to bottom and back again about once every two minutes. Tetley's gears performed well, but annoyed me all the same. Now, the bicycle is a wonderful invention, not least because its basic design has remained unchanged for so long. Gears are also a wonderful invention, for by some inscrutable process they allow me to pedal up slopes that should be beyond me. At least *I* can't scrute the process – and that's my point. I'm not an engineer, I'm a cyclist or, to use the current idiom, a user – which makes me sound like some kind of addict. The thing that irritated this user about Tetley's gears is that on the left handlebar the smaller of the two levers let me go slower, while on the right handlebar the smaller one let me go faster. 'Slow' is a small sort of idea – small turns of the pedal, small bits of ground covered per turn – so surely the small lever should mean slower on *both* sides. The solution to this mystery lies, I'm sure, in the identity of the designer of these gear levers. He or she has done an excellent functional job – they work – but a poor ergonomic job. I bet *they* can scrute how the gears work; I bet they know that the smallest cog on one end of the chain lets you go slowest while the smallest cog on the other end lets you go fastest. This is design by how the thing works rather than by how it's used. Small point, but rationalising my irritation got me through the worst of the draining and by the right turn at Aird of Coigach it had stopped.

Just after the turn, on a walk-up slope miles from anywhere, I passed a solitary young woman walking in the opposite direction with a small pack. Her 'Hyeallo!' was distinctly Eastern European and I wondered where she'd come from. It could have been from the mysterious green sheds where the road bridged the River Polly. They were easily the largest structure for miles around, were extremely well maintained and had a large number of men working in and around them… but their use, or even ownership, was a mystery to me, as not a single sign was to be seen anywhere near them. MOD?

Unwarranted suspicion is probably another symptom of remotitis and so, to keep me occupied as far as Inverkirkaig, I did a mental calculation for Inverpolly, which is where the mysterious sheds were, and came up with a remoteness of R = 5: 'in the sticks'. Fair enough.

Actually, the scenery suddenly kept me occupied too. A rapid descent from the misty mountains turfed me out unexpectedly on a captivating corner of Enard Bay, where the smell of seaweed and a rare hint of sunshine combined to get me out of the saddle and sitting on a low roadside wall to take in the first close sight of the sea since Ullapool. Seagulls and oystercatchers noisily competed for food exposed by the receding tide, sighing wavelets rustled the edge of the seaweed carpet and, in the distance, a scatter of randomly dropped islets pushed inviting mounds of bracken out of a sea that now glistened in the sunshine. Behind me every car that passed – and that's not many – also slowed to take in the view until pushed along by the car behind, for this was still a single-track road. There was nowhere for them to park and it's a shame my next stop – a scheduled one for coffee – wasn't located here.

Achins Book Shop and Coffee Shop at Inverkirkaig is described on a local website as 'possibly the remotest book shop in Britain' and so, as a fan of books, cafes and remoteness, I just had to call in. Their car park beside the rushing River Kirkaig was packed and there were lots of folk in boots milling about, but I couldn't see any book shop or indeed any building. My attention was finally caught by a sign that pointed up an unfeasibly steep slope to a grey shed in an anonymous yard and so I pushed Tetley up what I was sure would be the steepest up-slope on this trip. At the top it was clear that the only building there was this shed, although it seemed to have neither door nor window. Another sign pointed me up the sort of side alley you expect to be swimming in last night's vomit and there I parked Tetley (in the alley – there was no vomit). Squeezing through one of the two doors, I found myself in another Celtic Suicide Cafe.

I think the CD wafting its sorrowful strains over the room was called *Scottish Moods* and it had evidently already had its effect on customers and staff, who all stared glumly in front of them as though they still had most of a life sentence to serve. It was steamingly hot and I noisily removed my cycling equipment before approaching the counter with a cheery 'Hello!'

'Ugh,' said the grey-ponytailed male assistant.

'Nice day for a bike ride.'

'Ugh.'

'Er, a cup of coffee, please, and… what are these scones called?'

'Ugh… scones.'

'And a scone then, please.'

'Ugh. Ugh.'

Maybe he'd had a bad morning. The coffee was fine, the scone delicious and the book shop excellent indeed but, given that they'd gone to the effort of investing in such a spectacular area, I just don't get their failure to make the most of it. Steps up to the building maybe? A window onto something other than a wall, e.g. the view? A CD that makes you want to buy it rather than rip it out, jump on it and cast it into the Minch? Anyway, the place was there and I'm glad it was.

Before mounting up again, I turned over the sheet in my map case and was surprised to see this page finally ending in the blue of a northern sea, across which two magic words were printed in italics: Cape Wrath. It's difficult to say which emotion was the stronger: the sudden realisation that I would probably achieve my goal or the tinge of disappointment that these days spent on the open road would soon end. More immediately, I took in the latest local details revealed by the map and set off. Crossing the River Kirkaig, I'd slipped not only into Assynt, another vast area of spectacular mountain scenery (still invisible today, though – I think that cloud there hides Suilven and that one Canisp), but also out of the old Rossshire and into the old Sutherland – though still in the giant modern county of 'Highland', of course.

The name Sutherland comes from 'southern land', a rather surprising name given where we are... but it was the Norsemen who named it as the land to the south of the Orkneys.

More MacTwaddle

The old county of Sutherland offers a simple case study of how Britain still hasn't managed to shake off the idiocies of the feudal system.

You'll remember from the rainy day in Appin that, from around the twelfth century, the King of Scotland, when he stopped being merely King of the Scots, started handing out property to clan chiefs as though it was his to hand out. A clan chief granted property by the king was called a thane and the said property a thanedom. Rankwise, one thane equalled about half an earl.

The thanedom of Sutherland was granted by King David around 1230 (over lunch, perhaps?) to the chief of the Murray clan, a chap who, oddly enough, was not called Murray but Mr Freskin de Moravia. Freskin had earned the honour by chasing the Norsemen and a few assorted villains out of Sutherland. Now, in a sane (as opposed to thane) system the award would have died with the one who earned it, but old Freskin's family carried on benefiting from his personal achievements until the very moment I am writing this and, odds-on, the moment you are reading it.

His descendants, or those who married his descendants, eventually ditched the thilly thane title to become Earls of Sutherland and then Dukes of Sutherland. Their local pile was at Dunrobin Castle over on the east coast, but they also owned land in England, including Trentham Hall in the Potteries and what was regarded as the most valuable of all private residences in nineteenth-century London: Stafford House, later renamed Lancaster House and now owned by the government. In 1880 the incumbent Duke owned about half a million hectares and, unsurprisingly, another was a major tenant-evictor in the Clearances.

The current holder of the title is Elizabeth Millicent Jansen, Countess of Sutherland and still clan chief of the Murrays – but still, you'll notice, not actually called Murray.

What a pile of MacTwaddle this all is.

Sutherland was probably the county worst affected by the Clearances. While even neighbouring counties slightly increased their total population over the nineteenth century, from 1801 to 1901 Sutherland's total resident population actually fell from a mere 23,117 to an even merer 21,440. It's the only old Scottish county with no town at all – and I'd say that makes it the only one in Great Britain, too, as even Rutland's got Oakham. It's also said to have the lowest population density in Western Europe, although I'd have thought that this sort of statement needs to include a definition of what kind of administrative area you're using.

A fair few of today's Sutherlanders live in the next settlement en route, Lochinver, which I approached past the tall, unsympathetic storage units of its small fishing harbour. With its barking dogs, wailing children and overweight mothers, Lochinver might better be named Council Estate on Sea and I scuttled through as fast as I could. To the passing cyclist, Clachtoll – where my wiggly route once again struck the coast – looked just as bad, but Julie told me later that she spent a happy half-hour here paddling on the beach under a balmy afternoon sun (probably the same break in the weather I'd experienced at Enard Bay) and so I wouldn't place too much weight on my cursory assessments. Clachtoll's neighbour Stoer had a spectacularly sited but ruined church and below it a very stern modern wall hiding the old graveyard almost completely. The explanation appeared just beyond the wall: a field pockmarked with hundreds of rabbit holes whose inhabitants must have been judged to be unwelcome visitors to the cemetery. Stoer lends its name to a small peninsula to the north of our route, at the end of which sits Cluas Deas, one of the five major lighthouses along this west coast together with those at the Mull of Kintyre, Ardnamurchan, Rubha Reigh (north of Gairloch) and Cape Wrath.

This last stretch of the day, on the relentlessly undulating single-track B869, was testing my muscles to the limit and, while on another day I'd have stopped off at the inviting beach of Clashnessie, with its golden sands and proper, crashing waves, I pressed on – with tonight's shower, food and bed firmly in my mental sights. Clashnessie used to be a crofting community at least twice as big as now and included a 'black house', one of the traditional dwellings in this area comprising a single room housing humans at one end and their livestock at the other. A pretty warm arrangement, I would think.

Just before my destination I caught a glimpse across the fields of Oldany Island. Like most of the features along the route, I'd looked up Oldany Island on the 'Gazetteer for Scotland' website before my trip and found that its last entry, in 2004, recorded an area of 200 hectares, a population of nil and a tourist rating of nil. Rather harsh, I think. Like the entry for Earth in *The Hitch Hiker's Guide to the Galaxy*, which was eventually edited from 'harmless' to 'almost harmless', I hope one day Oldany Island's tourist rating may sneak up to 'almost nil'.

Struggling over a final hill, I spotted Julie in the distance, waving me on to the Drumbeg Hotel. This hotel's owners, yet another couple from the north of England, told us that they were two years into a ten-year plan to improve this already excellent hostelry, but I hope they retain most of the original atmospheric features, especially the tremendous period piece of the wood-panelled reception area, which looked just like the sort of place you'd be happy to pitch up on a freezing winter's night in, say, 1953 – especially if your name's Hannay and you'd just risked life and limb clambering across the girders of the Forth Road Bridge in search of 'The Thirty-Nine Steps'. In other words, it felt satisfyingly remote – and two clear cases of remotitis underlined the point. (For the Drumbeg Hotel itself R = 4, but would be much higher in its environs.)

First, as we gawped across the wilderness from the dining room, a small saloon car pulled up with a child dangling perilously out of the passenger window, its harassed mother gabbling at it from the driver's seat. (It was so quiet we could hear the gabbling from within the hotel.) The child, revealed as a boy of about seven, sprang out and proceeded to make his way to the hotel via the inside of a swinging metal sign that stood by the road to engage the passing motorist. Mother, carrying eggs, took a more standard path and noisily denounced the route taken by her offspring. Both soon re-emerged eggless, son taking the same metal-clanging route, mother again finding fault with it. Once in the car, the engine of which had been left running, they disappeared into the night, mother still complaining of her son's reckless behaviour, son still hanging half-in and half-out of the car. No seat belts were used.

Second, our charming dinner waitress had certainly contracted a serious case of remotitis, as revealed by her responses to our every request:

'Lasagne, please.'

'Hhyyyeee… yes. And for you, sir?'

'Fish and chips, I think.'

'Hhyyyeee… yes, of course. And to drink?'

'Two more glasses of Merlot, I think.'

'Hhyyyeee… two wines. Hhyyyeeeee!'

Each 'hhyyyeee' was accompanied by a broad grin that said, I think, 'Yes, and aren't we just lucky to be alive and well and right here tonight?'

Yes, indeed.

Chapter 15

The Final Straight: Eddrachillis Bay to the Kyle of Durness

The next morning saw me up and about before breakfast to stroll round the village of Drumbeg. It took about three minutes – and two of those were spent reading the exotic offerings listed outside the delicatessen that doubles as Drumbeg Stores and Post Office. They included 'Rannoch Smoked Goose', 'Taste of Gigha Cheese', 'Wild Boar Terrine' and 'Smoked Olive Tapenade'. This was a recent winner of the title 'Best Village Shop in Scotland', as judged by the Countryside Alliance, *Farmer's Weekly* and the *Daily Telegraph*. Given the competition, this is seriously impressive stuff. Just as in the rest of the UK, rural post offices here have been under threat of closure and their numbers had already fallen dramatically; the response of many that I'd used on this journey had been to sell everything under the sun and Drumbeg's was evidently a first-class example of this.

Alas, I'd be unable to prove it as I had to be away before they opened. After touring the rest of village, at least the rest that I could see – a church, a handful of houses and a phone box – I joined Julie for breakfast, where we had a front-row view of the community's entire early morning activity: the arrival of the post bus, the last post collection of the day (7.45 a.m.), the boarding of two passengers (half of Drumbeg's resident population, I shouldn't wonder) and its departure.

After that, the next item of traffic was yours truly – thirty minutes later. For me, among all the positive attributes of most Highland settlements I passed through, this is the most endearing: that between, say, 7.30 p.m. and 7.30 a.m. there's almost nothing on the main road through town. There's nowhere else to go, you see, and anyone who's coming is already here. Priceless.

So it was in a light and expansive mood that I left Drumbeg to resume my circuit of the B869. It took less than two miles for my mood to change.

This stretch, just in from the coast, was so consistently hilly that not only did I walk Tetley up all the up-slopes, but also walked him down nearly all the down-slopes, such was the severity of the gradients. Every vehicle overtaking me downhill left a whiff of burnt rubber in the air, including the one with a dead deer slung across its trailer. Julie later showed me a tape from a video camera strapped to the headrest of the Golden Toyota's passenger seat and all you could see were alternate shots of sky and tarmac – plus one quick flash of a struggling cyclist's straining calves. On the very steepest of steep up-slopes, which may well have been the one out of Nedd, the next village, I passed the time by roughly calculating my walking speed from the frequency of my steps and the length of my feet (since, as I pressed Tetley onward, the toes of one all but touched the heel of the other) and it came to more or less one mile an hour. Lest anyone doubt me, I took a photo of the offending slope and subsequently applied a dusty old protractor to the photo, which showed the angle to be 27 degrees and therefore the slope to be a smidgen off 30 per cent (or 1-in-3.3). What I found odd was that a long way after this and after several similar slopes, The Highland Council made its only signposted gradient announcement of the morning by alerting the wary road-user to a 25 per cent gradient ahead. 25 per cent?! Ha – kids' stuff!

The last two days had been 44 miles apiece and today's was due to be pretty much the same, and so spending several hours to cover the first eight miles might lead to 'an undoing' later in the day. We'd see. Press on.

This corner of Sutherland is dominated by the giant bulk of Quinag, one of the spectacular mountains created in the Torridonian sandstone at the time of the Moine Thrust. Quinag boasts a rare triple statistic. I'd heard of a category of Scottish mountain called the Munro (a peak over 3,000 feet, or around 900 metres), but until this trip I'd never heard of a Corbett – except for Ronnie, Harry and Harry H., of course. A Corbett is a Scottish peak of at least 2,500 feet (760 metres) which drops at least 500 feet (150 metres) on all sides. No, really: there have been people on this planet with nothing better to do than dream up arbitrary categories of mountain shape, naming the shape after themselves, and J. Rooke Corbett was one of them, Hugh Munro another. Of course, there are other people who've got nothing better to do than take the mickey out of them. If you're over 1.75 metres tall, weigh over 70 kilograms and couldn't give more than 2.0 hoots about Scottish mountain categories, then I define us both as Mickeys.

Pushing up to the top of another killer slope, this Mickey was within two miles of three towering Corbetts, for Quinag is an astonishing three-Corbetts-in-one feature. Alas, I couldn't savour it as the day was another low-cloud affair and, although I could see the sides of the mountain thrusting dramatically into the greyness, there was no way of knowing where they stopped – heaven, for all I could tell. I rested on a bench, thoughtfully provided by Greult Dijkstra and Willemina Wolfers on their fiftieth wedding anniversary in 2001, and pondered the nature of views (the nature of anything but my throbbing knees and aching back, in fact). It occurred to me that countryside views in general comprise mostly horizontals – cloud layers, horizons, lake shores, hedgerows etc. – while townscapes tend to comprise verticals – walls, windows, signposts, double-decker buses, traffic lights, people. And also that horizontal is our resting position, while vertical is our active position. And further, that maybe this explains why most of us feel more relaxed in the country: horizontal = good, vertical = bad. I'm pretty sure I was suffering from RSSS – Repetitive Scottish Scenery Syndrome. Or possibly remotitis. Squirting some cold water over my head, I trudged on.

The last mile of the B869 before it joins the main road north, the A894, is the only stretch on this trip owned and managed by the John Muir Trust. John Muir was a pioneering Scottish-born conservationist, one of the first people to campaign for the active protection of wild places. The trust which he inspired owns large tracts of land in some of the remotest parts of Scotland, including parts of Knoydart that I'd stared longingly at from the Skye ferry. This stretch is the northern tip of the Trust's 34,000-hectare Quinag Estate, purchased in 2005. The John Muir Trust website (www.jmt.org) is worth visiting for its photographs alone.

Eventually the B-road punishment was over and I celebrated my reunion with civilisation by pulling into the first lay-by for coffee next to an Austrian camper van, before crossing Loch a' Chàirn Bhàin via the Kylesku Bridge. Opened in 1984, this dramatic, curving structure, built on two pairs of V-shaped legs, was designed by Arup (a firm, not a bloke), won several prizes and now saves the weary commuter who lives in Kylesku but works in Kylestrome no less than 97 miles on their journey to work. Now over twenty years old, the bridge is already looking a little care-worn but its span is just as dramatic. The ferry it replaced, by the way, had for much of its life been a free one. Its last representative was the *Maid of Glencoul*, which I'd seen moored that rainy September morning when crossing Loch Linnhe, where it formed the backup vessel for the Corran ferry.

In crossing the bridge I was entering MacKay country – the last of the tea-towel clans. The MacKays greeted me with yet another killer gradient and, while pushing Tetley ever northward, I heard a certain rhythmic grunting from behind: whu whoo, whu whoo, whu whoo, whu whoo – today's first cyclists, two of them, out of the saddle and taking years off the useful life of their knees. Before I could decide whether to say 'Keep it up, lads!' or 'Take a break, lads!', they'd whu-whooed passed me with a 'Yer' each and were gone: two black-clad young men with halfway-up-Everest faces. John o'Groats by teatime?

The rest of the session till lunch was occupied by a pleasant enough meander through the Loch a' Mhuilinn National Reserve, the most northerly remnant of native oak woodland in the British Isles. Never having been this far into the North-West Highlands, I was expecting treeless, wind-swept landscapes to the horizon, but this all looked like standard Highland fare: lumpy, lake-strewn uplands, broken by forests sweeping down to the sea. Badcall Bay came and went. The authorities claim the name comes from the Gaelic for 'thicket-dropping' but, never having witnessed anyone on any occasion dropping a thicket – or even being caught in possession of a thicket – I tend to the more obvious argument that trying to land a boat into that rocky inlet would be a jolly bad call indeed.

A better call would be Scourie Bay. The little settlement of Scourie is really two in one, the first on the hill with the school and the second down by the bay with the caravans and the Anchorage, where I laid my own for lunch. This was no Celtic Suicide Cafe, but a normal one, with normal, crackly country and western music, normal woolly-hatted locals, greeting the visiting cyclist with wry comments on his likely insanity, and a normal Eastern European waitress. Mind you, my soup did come with an After Eight (it was 1.15 p.m.).

A few more ups and downs took me to Laxford Bridge where the road from Lairg, Inverness and the rest of the world comes in from the east. The horrors of the B869 had taught me a useful lesson in up and downing and I offer it as the Fifth and Final Law of Cycle Touring:

5: When you hit the lily pond, you're at the top.

On the ascent little lochans with water flowing through them come and go, but the one at the top that just sits there with still corners, whose water hasn't moved since water was invented, attracts water lilies – often whole bank-to-bank carpets of them. With the help of this knowledge I bounced through Sutherland's remaining little testers pretty happily.

The clouds were finally lifting a little and, of the two peaks that now filled the eastern horizon, one was actually clear to the top: Arkle. Its northern neighbour, still in the clammy grip of heaven's cloudy claw, was Foinaven. If these names are as familiar to you as to me, it's because a slightly misspelt Foinavon won the 1967 Grand National at 100-1, while Arkle, more often a favourite, never won it. These would be the fast-moving steeds rather than slow-moving mountains. Time for a little more geology, I think.

Gneiss one, Lewis

The surface rocks around here include what's known as the Lewisian Gneiss.

Gneiss is a metamorphic rock, i.e. one created by the forces of heat and pressure, and comprises a crystalline mixture of quartz, feldspar, mica and hornblende. It's called Lewisian because the largest outcrops of this age occur on the Isle of Lewis.

And it's age that matters. The Lewisian Gneiss contains rocks that are not only the oldest in the UK but some of the oldest in the world – at a literally unimaginable 3,000 million years old.

Now, some of you paying attention at the front of the class may find something odd in that. If the orientation of much of the Highlands was caused by faults 400 million years ago, including the Moine Thrust, and the volcanoes of Ardnamurchan were caused by ocean creation 60 million years ago, how can it be that these rocks in north-west Scotland are much, much older than that?

The answer is that when they were created they weren't in Scotland. They were created by the heat and pressure several miles under the earth's surface, in fact quite probably under the southern hemisphere's surface, and appear at the surface here and now (and, incidentally, in Scandinavia, Greenland and Canada) only because of all the subsequent processes, of which we've had just a glimpse.

I don't know about you, but I find this quite amazing – not only that it's happened, but also that we know it has.

For the afternoon's first break, I pulled in at a lay-by giving a picture-postcard view along Loch Laxford. The rough grass leading to the shore was speckled with tiny yellow flowers that waved brightly in front of the rich browns of the seaweed exposed by the tide. Barely a ripple broke the smooth surface of the loch on which no boat was to be seen, although a small white rowing boat sat expectantly at the head of a slipway a hundred metres away. In the distance the underlying white rock of the successive headlands pushed through the sparse grass to add regular white reflections to the light blues of Loch Laxford as it stretched out to the open North Atlantic in the far distance.

Into this still and timeless world came the sudden braking scrape of a Saab 93, out of whose driver's seat leapt a breathless thirty-something male, camera already half-raised. Before the unchanging view and my unblinking stare, his aim, click and withdrawal were executed in rapid succession, followed swiftly by re-entry, belt-up, de-brake and screeching re-launch. The whole manoeuvre had taken less than thirty seconds – and that included the gravel resettling. My contemplation broken, I pulled Tetley from his resting place and set off again myself.

The terrain still provided sharp gradients and rapidly changing views as the A838 followed a switchback route from one valley to the next. On the last stretch from Rhiconich to Durness, however, the trees finally disappeared, the scenery calmed down and the desolate views across wild moorland that I'd been expecting finally opened up, at least to the west. To the east, Foinaven still glowered under low cloud. Near the top of the road, which had to that point been free from both buildings and humans, an isolated lake opened up to the east, bearing a small boat with three figures standing in it. Opposite this a house – or possibly, from its size, a hotel – was under construction and surrounded by noisy activity. Very soon after, there was peace again.

Julie had already called with the good news that the final section is a long, steady downhill and I was required neither to pedal nor brake for mile after delicious mile. Being on a single-track road, though, I *was* required by etiquette to raise a regular righthand to passing cars either because they'd waited in a passing place or because I had and they'd waved their thanks to me. A local friend tells us that this 'Highland wave' has become such a reflex that she finds herself waving to everyone she passes in the street – while just walking. Another friend tells the story of her childhood visits to the Highlands in the back of her parents' car, when every parental wave was explained as a greeting to their old friend, Mrs MacAllister. Even now, when due to drive up here, she still looks forward to 'waving to Mrs MacAllister'.

The last three miles revealed the beautiful Kyle of Durness to my left. This sandy tidal tongue of the Atlantic separates one of Britain's last empty quarters from the rest of the world. Over the sands on the left bank lay the Parbh (pronounced 'Parve'), the isolated peninsula whose northernmost corner forms Cape Wrath, my final objective and the target for tomorrow's ride.

The end of today's was the Cape Wrath ferry terminal at Keoldale, where Julie waved me in and where we hauled Tetley into the Golden Toyota, which had been easy to spot in the distance for a good couple of miles. After sharing the highlights of our days, which in Julie's case had already included a whistle-stop tour of Durness, we looked around the deserted ferry terminal.

I say 'ferry terminal' but what actually occupied the map coordinates where the ferry is marked as terminating were a slipway, a plastic shelter and a bright yellow noticeboard. This latter contained many printed details of the ferry's operations, across which were scrawled in black felt-tip a number of caveats relating to tides and days of the week, plus the following:

THURSDAY. SORRY. DUE TO VISIBILITY NO
MORE TRIPS TODAY.

We could easily see the other side: the visibility was fine. We'd allowed just one day's contingency and had to be southbound by Sunday at the very latest; all our hopes really lay on a crossing to Capeside tomorrow. A nervousness swept over us, but I tried to hide it behind a carefree comment: 'I suppose the book could be called *From the Mull to the Keoldale Slipway*.' It didn't raise a laugh.

*

A little subdued, we drove off through Durness to the Smoo Cave Inn.

Durness prides itself on being the 'most north-westerly' community in Great Britain, but – and I may be putting my head on a risky geographical block here – I'm pretty sure that such a concept makes no sense. 'Most northerly' makes sense (Skarfskerry near John o'Groats, actually) and 'most westerly' (Kilchoan on Ardnamurchan, of course); but what does 'most north-westerly' mean? Does it have to be on some 45-degree line from somewhere? From where? At any rate, it's definitely the last settlement on my journey and their website had assured me that I'd be offered *ceud mile failte* ('a hundred thousand welcomes'). That would be about 312 from each of the 320 inhabitants then. Better brace myself.

On the face of it, Durness doesn't have a lot going for it, but – with one exception – it makes the best of what it's got and actually I quite like the place.

In Balnakiel Bay it has a mile and a half of golden, sandy beach which, being on the very edge of the North Atlantic, sitting within striking distance of the Arctic Circle and facing west, ought to be a write-off for bathers but, truth to tell, when we were there it was both warm and glitteringly idyllic, a combination that had attracted about 60 paddlers, 30 of whom were expansively mooing cows, 25 loudly complaining oystercatchers ('Squeet! Hey, cow, your space is that field, our space is this beach! Squeet!') and the remainder humans.

In Smoo Cave it has a fantastically huge cavern that's signed, stepped and walkwayed by solid wooden installations with EU subsidy oozing from every joint.

And in an anonymous white bungalow on a Sangomore hillside it has a blue-chip Beatles link as this is the house where little John Lennon used to come and spend summer holidays with the Sutherlands (his mother's sister's husband's family). His lyrics for 'In My Life' (1965) recall places he remembered and, according to the notice in Durness's John

Lennon Memorial Garden, these places were in Durness. It certainly meant something to him as he brought Yoko up here four years later. Wandering around the garden, I appreciated the symmetry of having a Beatles connection both at the start and end of this journey. The garden had only recently opened but I felt it was destined to be a magnet for Lennon fans. Its creators may find they've included a somewhat unnecessary introduction that identifies John Lennon as 'the singer/songwriter with the famous 1960s group The Beatles, who went on to pursue a major solo career'. Oh, *that* John Lennon.

The exception to the rule in Durness is the former Cape Wrath Hotel. At the time of writing, its website is still alive and kicking and it was for this reason that I'd tried to book in there, but a phone call had announced it as closed and a glance at the sombre reality instantly confirmed this. Its site is clearly the ideal location in Durness estate agents' terms. A substantial structure, it sits astride a small rise in Keoldale to take in the whole panorama of the Kyle of Durness, the majestic mountains beyond, the deserted green slopes of the Parbh, the route of the ferry crossing and, at the very foot of its drive, the Keoldale slipway itself. It's surely where all Cape Wrath seekers (and, as we'll see, they do exist) would want to stay. So what went wrong? Well, according to one of several informants that Julie seemed to have built up during her short stay here, a new set of owners did just about everything wrong that hotel proprietors could possibly do wrong and, when this prompted the hotel's loss of its fishing and hunting licences, well, the writing was firmly on the quayside. It was recently sold and is now a private house.

So the Smoo Cave Inn it was for us. First impressions weren't great: a child racing a barely controlled quad bike around the car park took one look at me and pronounced: 'F**k! This f**kin' quad's shite!' He was about eight. Second impressions – a room with no hooks to hang clothes on and an outside wall on the inside – fell into the 'to be decided' category. Third impressions, after an excellent 'haggis, neaps and tatties' plus a passable pint in the bar were very good. Almost a normal pub, with normal irascible locals at the bar and normal Eastern European staff behind it, the Smoo Cave Inn had that edge of eccentricity that reminded us we were on the very edge of Great Britain: a giant gaming machine whose display would probably be more visible to shipping than the Cape Wrath light, a pool table cleverly positioned so that at some point in the game every one of the seated diners would receive the blunt end of a cue in their haggis, and two or three positively huge local girls whose fingers were capable only of choosing three jukebox tracks at a time. On the whole, I'd recommend the Smoo Cave Inn.

Oh, and if you need countable sheep to help you fall into slumber, just open the bedroom curtains and you'll find an infinite supply.

Chapter 16

The Grim Cape: The Parbh and Cape Wrath

Nearly 700 years before the final day of my trip, the King of France had thousands of Knights Templar arrested and tortured. That bad day for the KTs was Friday the thirteenth of October 1307 and it's one explanation as to why, on subsequent Friday the thirteenths, some people still worry that something bad's going to happen to them. Another explanation is that they're all daft. What these people have, apparently, is paraskavedekatriaphobia. Well, I don't – and the thought of a parakeet playing records in a cave not only failed to frighten me this Friday the thirteenth but hardly occurred to me at all as I pulled on the cycling togs for what I was confident would be the last time on this trip.

Down at Keoldale, an empty stage awaited its players. The choppy kyle slapped at an empty quay, the old hotel reached towards ragged clouds and the shelter, perched on its small hummock, rocked in the wind. Julie and I pulled up to check if any more felt-tip had been applied to the ferry notice. No, so far so good – though no sign of a ferry.

Next on the scene was a narrow, ageing saloon car driven by a wide, ageing man in a blue sailing cap. After he'd parked it in one of two official slots, squeezed out, inspected the sea and lit an unfeasibly long cigar, I asked him about the chances of the ferry running today.

'No' bad,' he offered in a north of England accent. ''Appen John'll be 'ere soon.'

So Captain Havana wasn't the ferryman.

Next on the scene was a southern couple who joined us in the shelter, after which the scene filled up pretty quickly: a brace of Germans, three northern hostellers and a Scandinavian family with better English than all of us. Each arrival, with much eyebrow-raising and chin-rubbing, looked up at the clouds and down at the sea. None of us could see any sign of the ferry. While we were waiting, the northerners told me that two young, black-clad cyclists had stayed at the youth hostel last night – so the two whu-whooers of Kylesku had cycled no further than me after all. Finally, a muddy Land Rover pulled into the other official slot and, to a barrage of encouraging smiles, out stepped John the Ferryman. After a hushed conversation with Captain Havana, plus some more extravagant chin-rubbing, he marched up to the knot of would-be Capesiders to announce:

'Aye, the ferry'll be running today.'

And then, after assessing the state of the landlubbing rabble:

'I'll be pulling her up at the slipway, not this shelter.'

With that, the ferryman climbed down to a rubber dinghy and rowed out to a tiny, red and white craft called *Fiona* – so small that we'd all overlooked it. *Fiona the Cape Wrath Ferry*, which instantly entered my Ferry Top Ten just above the *MV Coruisk* at Mallaig, runs daily from May to September, subject to weather, sea conditions and one even more important factor, which I was to encounter just a couple of miles beyond the far shore. It links with a minibus, stabled Capeside, which transfers the bulk of the passengers to the Cape. No ferry, no minibus; no minibus, no ferry. It turned out that yesterday's poor visibility had been not on the Kyle of Durness but at Cape Wrath itself, where the view, I took it, was the thing and an invisible view would mean a frustrated busload.

Once the ferryman, Captain Havana, a girl on Cape business and Tetley had been stowed on board, there was room for just six more of us pressed into the vessel's passenger cabin – that is to say, the entire vessel. The six did not include Julie, who had opted to follow on a later crossing. This crossing was brisk and bracing and consisted almost entirely of the ferryman collecting fares with his one spare hand. Change was out of the question and every note passing hands was a mere finger grip away from being deposited in the Bank of the North Atlantic. Fares were very reasonable and return only – there being no other way of getting back. Well, almost. There is a very long walk along the west coast of the Cape via Sandwood Bay to Kinlochbervie, but anyone attempting this would be well advised to take camping gear and alert the ferry operator to their plans.

Having landed half a minibusload, the ferry went back for the other half while I set off up the hill on the eleven-mile run across the deserted Parbh, keeping an eye open for wildlife unused to vehicles on the narrow track. The first life – wild or not – was a dusty saloon car about half a mile from the quayside and heading in the opposite direction, with a young woman at the wheel. The next a young man in sunglasses atop a quad bike also heading Durness-wards. Soon after this I stood aside while the dirty white minibus, with Captain Havana at the wheel and a dozen waving, bobbing passengers behind, overtook me, heading for the Cape. And after that, silence.

The single-track road, now grassy and pockmarked, was built in 1828 to access the new lighthouse. Pre-Clearances, there used to be three settlements strung along this west shore of the Kyle: Portover, Geachreamh and Aldan. By the 1930s there were still about 35 people living Capeside, plus the lighthouse-keepers. Nowadays, Julie's informants assured her that the permanent population is exactly zero. (Those early passers-by must have been overnighters headed back to the rest of the world.) This is in an area of eighty square miles, all of which is now moorland and a Site of Special Scientific Interest.

Signs of habitation and activity still remain, though. In the first two miles I passed three substantial houses, all of which looked to be still occasionally inhabited, plus various bits and pieces of machinery. In fact, so few were the previous residents that pretty well every stick and stone on the road, ruined or not, is explained on the local website: www.capewrath.org.uk.

The most eye-catching structures on the Parbh, though, are unmissable – indeed were specifically built to be unmissable. They're designed in black, white and yellow checks and stand beside similarly gaudy barriers. For nowadays the Parbh is a military firing range.

When scheduled, the Ministry of Defence's exercises close the whole of Capeside to the public and this is the final factor in whether the ferry runs or not. Their key point seems to be target practice and the target they practise on is Garve Island (*An Garbh-eilean*), lying just off the north coast about halfway between Durness and Cape Wrath. Judging from the state of the road, three miles away at its nearest, they need that practice. One of the houses I passed, opposite Loch Inshore, is owned by the MOD: it's the one with the empty bottle of Cabernet Sauvignon in the window. Exercises are not permitted until after the lambing season and this year no more were due until after the end of the ferrying season – and so the barriers were open.

It was a solitary but jolly enough ride across the Parbh. The wind had eased, the rain held off yet again and the barren landscape regularly changed its angle and shade as the clouds thinned and then thickened again in their eastward wander. Barren it was at last: not a tree to be seen outside the occasional valleys and even there just scrubby shrubs. Sheep came and went in bunches, the ubiquitous black-headed gulls squeaked the odd squeak and an occasional rabbit scuttled out of my path. But apart from that the only moving thing was me and the only sound the click-rattle-click of Tetley's gears.

Progress towards the Cape is measured by regular mileposts and with about four to go I pulled up in surprise at a T-junction. No sign indicated which way to Cape Wrath, although a sign facing the opposite way did warn of the weight limit on a bridge I'd recently crossed – a warning to whom I can't say, as the only way to have driven here would have been across that very bridge. A glance at the map told me that right would be the way to Kervaig House, on a small bay reputed to have been a favourite Norse landing spot. The house is now used by the Mountain Bothies Association which, as I'm sure I don't need to tell you, is responsible for the upkeep of a hundred or so bothies scattered about the UK. I needed to tell me, though, as I'm afraid I'd had to look up 'bothy', discovering that it's a rough-and-ready shelter for hikers. And I suppose an intrusive bothy manager would be a busybothy. I later learned that two of today's minibus passengers were dropped off here to stay at the Kervaig bothy for two nights.

Just after turning left and remounting, I found myself demounting again to let Captain Havana and his brood bounce past once more on their way back down to the ferry. By my calculations this would give me a good hour of solitude at the Cape before he was back with the next load, an hour during which I felt duty-bound to reflect on these last sixteen cycling days on the edge of wilderness and let you in on the meaning of life. Actually, no, I don't know why people say that – that they're off to India or Ilkley Moor to find the meaning of life – because obviously there isn't one. What I felt was floating about just below the surface, though, and what would probably be revealed unto me as I tucked into my raspberry jam sandwiches on Cape Wrath, was more a philosophy of life, an approach, an attitude that allows you to make the best of it.

I was certainly looking forward to the views anyway, as I'd read many a reference to the 'feeling of boundless space', the 'unforgettable sight of the majestic cliffs', 'the thousands of wheeling seabirds' and so on, that were to be admired at the Cape. So it was with a slight frown that I looked up at the wispy, misty clouds slowly engulfing the hill ahead, beyond which lay the Cape.

My anticipation of an hour alone and stationary was also pricked by the sight of – of all things – a pedestrian, walking my way from the gates that mark the entrance to the lighthouse compound. He must have come round the west coast from Sandwood Bay. I know I should have stopped to chat, but the imminent achievement of my objective got the better of me and I just mumbled something about being pleased to see someone else exercising and pedalled on. With the walker's plaintive comment that there was no one else at the Cape ringing in my ear, I was away. Poor chap probably hadn't spoken to a soul for days.

I'm afraid I didn't look back as I pedalled onto the headland itself, applied my well-used brakes for the last time and slid to a triumphant halt by the low stone wall.

Mull 1, Cape 1.
Miles 586, Punctures 0.

*

There are only two 'capes' in Britain and they stand at
two extremes: Cape Cornwall and Cape Wrath. In fact,
I'd be so bold as to suggest that 'cape' means a headland
at an extremity, while 'mull' means a headland at the end
of a peninsula – though my dictionary makes no such
distinction. The Old Norse *hwarf* means 'turning point'
or 'cape'. This was Gaelicised as *parbh* and then anglicised
as 'wrath'. So Cape Wrath actually means Cape Cape. The
Gaelic for Cape Wrath, *Am Parbh*, is more sensible, meaning
simply 'The Cape'.

The lighthouse there, built in 1828 by Robert, the first
of the Stevensons, is the sixth I'd seen on this trip. You
may be eager to learn that the Cape Wrath light is white
and flashes every thirty seconds with the power of 204,000
candles. Not during the day, obviously. Its nominal range
is 24 miles and it has been an automatic light since 1998,
which means that the operation of the light is monitored
not from downstairs but from a desk over 200 miles away
in Edinburgh.

We haven't heard from Francis Groome and his friends
since Ullapool. At the start of this trip I quoted his
1882 description of the Mull of Kintyre as 'that dreaded
headland'. Well, the gloomy Groomster seemed to be in
equally sombre mood when he or his colleague washed up
here at 'the huge promontory of grim Cape Wrath'.

It was certainly pretty grim again today but whether or not it was a huge promontory was hard to tell, as low cloud and mist still clung to the cliffs, making their height – or rather depth – difficult to fathom, although I'm told that Clo Mòr cliffs, just a shade to the east of the Cape, are the highest sea cliffs in Great Britain. The sea itself, some 160 metres below, could occasionally be heard as a distant *swash* but could be seen only some way beyond the Cape as a vaguely flat, vaguely dark grey shape merging with the vaguely light grey shape of the clouds. (Vague or not, an invisible line extending seawards from the lighthouse finally converted shipping area Hebrides into shipping area Fair Isle.) I'd expected music of bird calls from the multitude of species – puffins, fulmars, razorbills, guillemots, kittiwakes – which, so said the guidebooks, have huge colonies in these high, remote cliffs. Nothing. Well, the occasional listless flap of a wandering gull, but essentially nothing. Approaching as near as I dare to the eastern edge of the Cape, I could pick out the top fifty metres or so of the cliff face opposite, but the only life to be seen was a single white bird of indistinguishable classification settling into its choice from about a hundred empty ledges.

Initially I found this unexpected silence rather disappointing, but it turns out that this was yet more evidence that I'm an unreconstructed townie. As the Sage later pointed out, birds do not hang around their nests merely for the benefit of the passing tourist but rather for the benefit of themselves and their offspring in – ah yes, I'd forgotten – the nesting season. Which happened to be already over. Fair comment, but even in the nesting season, fewer birds are nowadays seen here…

The seas they are a-changin'

Around the same time as I was puzzling over the silence at Cape Wrath, *The Times* was running an article with a possible explanation. You won't be surprised that the subject is once again global warming.

As I understand it, cold water in the North Sea sinks, causing a displacement that pulls in warmer water from across the Atlantic in what we call the Gulf Stream. This phenomenon is a traditional staple of Scottish travel guides that boast of mild, palm-fringed havens up on the west coast. However, nowadays the North Sea is not quite so cold, the displacement smaller, the Gulf Stream weaker and the seas off the west of Scotland… well, no, not exactly cooler but not so much warmer than seas elsewhere in Britain… because other factors are increasing temperatures. You're right – simple it ain't. Average sea temperatures around here had risen by about one degree Celsius over the previous seven years.

This had caused plankton and larvae to move away to the north, which in turn had drastically reduced the numbers of small shoaling fish and sand eels. These in their turn form the food for many seabirds, which had therefore either failed to breed or also moved further north. The alternative was starvation.

The Times article specifically discussed the far north of Scotland, breeding home to almost half of Europe's seabirds, and quoted an ecologist at the Royal Society for the Protection of Birds as being particularly worried about the Arctic skua which, he said, could disappear from British

> shores entirely. Another source focused on the similar plight
> of the kittiwake.
>
> The times, the seas and the cliffs are indeed a-changin'.

Apart from its silence, the walled compound in which Cape Wrath lighthouse stands reminded me of the one at the Point of Ardnamurchan: another disorderly jumble of ramshackle sheds, rusting equipment and undergrowth. A final calculation using the Scale of Remoteness seemed in order and came out exactly the same as at the Mull of Kintyre: R = 8, i.e. still not 'officially remote' but once again 'up shit creek'... which I certainly would have been if I didn't get back to that jetty in time.

Returning with a slight hint of haste, therefore, to where I'd propped Tetley against the corner of a tatty shed, I extracted the raspberry jam sandwiches lovingly prepared that morning at the Smoo Cave Inn and sat on a pile of old planks to ruminate.

The quiet and the absence of other humans also reminded me of the Mull of Kintyre and underlined the fact that I'd actually made it. A long time in the planning, sixteen days' actual cycling and about 600 miles under the tyres had seen me from one end of the Highlands to the other. I may not have adhered rigidly to The Rule, but as a device it had been useful in taking me to several out-of-the-way coastal spots that I otherwise might have ignored. To be honest with myself, it hadn't been until I'd turned onto the last map page at Inverkirkaig that I'd have put money on my getting all the way to Cape Wrath. While not exactly old, I was already some way over the hill, five or ten kilos overweight and by no means fit. A young cyclist would easily cover this route in a week, but if any older reader is considering this or any similar ride, then I have two lessons for them. The first is a physical one: the weight you carry is absolutely critical to the ease with which you'll achieve your goal. Quite apart from the moral boost Julie's support gave me, her transport of my kit over the last seven days made the going so much easier. The second is a mental one and is the same lesson I've applied many times: the only way to succeed in many challenges is one step at a time. One wheel turn at a time. A long bike ride is just a series of small bike rides.

Realising that this was as near as I was going to get to a philosophy of life, I'd started to gather my things together when an unexpected noise wafted in on the light breeze from the south.

Clatter...

??

Clatter brrrm...

Impossible.

Clatter brrrm chug clatter...

Through the gateway lurched the minibus. As it drew closer, I saw not Captain Havana at the wheel but another driver. Another driver, another minibus! Two minibuses stored Capeside threw all my calculations to the wind, cutting short my solitary reflections at the Cape. Of course, I was pleased to see Julie, who hugged me in congratulation, but my sanctuary was instantly invaded by a dozen unknowns, milling about my Cape and wandering off recklessly to the very edge of my cliffs. Oh well, I guess they'd paid their money too.

As for me, after a few photos, a wider wander round and another temporary farewell to Julie, I launched good old Tetley back down the track to civilisation, pondering other cyclable coasts in other lands. Are there ever clouds in Wales?

Statto Corner

In case anyone is tempted by these pages to embark on a similar journey, here are a few statistical titbits.

From the Mull to the Cape as the crow flies is 264 miles (425 kilometres). My route distance, calculated from maps and signposts rather than an odometer, was 586 miles (943 kilometres), i.e. over twice as far. The breakdown is as follows:

Day	From	To	Miles	Km	Comment
1	Mull of Kintyre	Campbeltown	21	34	Excludes getting to the Mull
2	Campbeltown	Tarbert	38	61	
3	Tarbert	Kilmartin	46	74	
4	Kilmartin	Oban	28	45	
5	Oban	Onich	41	66	
6	Onich	Sonachan	50	80	Via Corran ferry

Day	From	To	Miles	Km	Comment
7	Sonachan	Arisaig	53	85	
8	Arisaig	Avernish	40	64	Via Armadale ferry. Includes Kyle–Avernish diversion (9 ml / 14 km)
9	Avernish	Strathcarron	26	42	Includes Avernish–Kyle diversion (10 ml / 16 km)
10	Strathcarron	Applecross	22	35	
11	Applecross	Kinlochewe	42	68	
12	Kinlochewe	Mellon Charles	37	60	Includes Aultbea–Mellon Charles diversion (5 ml / 8 km)
13	Aultbea	Ullapool	44	71	
14	Ullapool	Drumbeg	44	71	
15	Drumbeg	Keoldale	43	69	
16	Keoldale	Cape Wrath	11	18	Via Cape Wrath ferry. Excludes returning from the Cape
		Total	586	943	

The average distance cycled was 38.5 miles (62 kilometres) a day, including the additional distance getting to the Mull and from the Cape. Average speed, from departure to arrival each day, i.e. including breaks, was a paltry 4.5 mph (7.2 kph).

I did it in three stages and used three ferries: Corran, Armadale and Cape Wrath.

Of the 16 days, rain fell on 8, of which 3 were almost complete washouts.

My average bed-and-breakfast cost was about £30 (at 2006/7 prices), but this could easily be reduced by using youth hostels and more bunkhouses.

Bike: Triban Trail 7 from Decathlon.

Other cyclists spotted en route: 30, i.e. an average of just 2 a day.

Off-road miles: 0.

Punctures: 0.

Words of Gaelic heard: 0.

Bibliography

Books

In some cases, I purposefully used old editions.

Automobile Association *AA Illustrated Guide to Britain's Coast* (1984, Drive Publications)

Connelly, Charlie *Attention All Shipping* (2004, Little, Brown Book Group)

Fairweather, Nicholas *Coasting Around Scotland* (2002, Cualann Press)

Groome, Francis Hindes (editor) *Ordnance Gazetteer of Scotland* (originally 1882, Thomas C. Jack. See also below)

Hendry, George *Midges in Scotland* (1989, Mercat Press)

Lister, John A. *The Scottish Highlands* (1977, John Bartholomew)

Lonely Planet *Lonely Planet Scotland* (2006, Lonely Planet Publications)

Murphy, Alan *Footprint Travel Guide: Scotland Highlands and Islands Handbook* (2005, Footprint Handbooks)

Salter, Paul *Bike Britain* (2002, Epic New Zealand Ltd)

Various *The Statistical Accounts of Scotland* (1791–9 and 1834–45, see below)

Ward Lock *Ward Lock Illustrated Guide Books: The Highlands of Scotland* (1937, Ward Lock)

Ward Lock *Ward Lock's Red Guide: Oban, Skye, Fort William, Western Highlands* (1962, Ward Lock)

Wester Ross Tourist Organisation *South-West Ross* (1970s, exact date unknown, Wester Ross Tourist Organisation)

Websites

www.edina.ac.uk/stat-acc-scot
The Statistical Accounts of Scotland

www.electricscotland.com
Especially good on history

www.geo.ed.ac.uk/scotgaz/gaztitle.html
Gazetteer for Scotland, a gazetteer of Scottish towns and villages, including Groome's 1882 *Ordnance Gazetteer of Scotland*, which is © The Editors of the Gazetteer for Scotland, 2002–2006

http://www.lhdigest.com/database/searchdatabase.cfm
World lighthouses

www.ordnancesurvey.co.uk/oswebsite/freefun/
didyouknow/placenames/gaelicglossary-a-b.html
Gaelic place names

www.railscot.co.uk
History of Scotland's railways

www.undiscoveredscotland.co.uk
Highly recommended reading, with some stunning photographs